Memoirs of a Cotswold Farmer's Boy

(Or Don't Try This at Home!)

Michael R Smith

Pen Press

First published in Great Britain by Pen Press

All paper used in the printing of this book has been made from wood grown in managed, sustainable forests.

ISBN13: 978-1-906710-21-7

Printed and bound in the UK
Pen Press is an imprint of Indepenpress Publishing Limited
25 Eastern Place
Brighton
BN2 1GJ

A catalogue record of this book is available from the British Library

Cover design by Jacqueline Abromeit

Preface

2008

One of our granddaughters, Georgia, came home from school saying that she had to write an essay about something her parents did when they were ten years old. If they could not think of anything, she could ask her grandparents. We fell for it, hook, line and sinker, and I produced two stories from my childhood. She took it to school, and the teacher enjoyed it so much that Georgia had to read it to the class, which caused much laughter.

This prompted my wife, Pat, to urge me to write down an account of my childhood for the grandchildren to read, ie Jess, Harley, Georgia, Bethany and Maia. They enjoyed it so much as bedtime reading (maybe it was giving them ideas of mischief-making) that I decided to enlarge it to include the rest of my life, in the hope of giving them and other people some amusement at my expense.

All the stories are true, for instance including Mr Plod in our dodgy activities. It was true, he used to give us a good hiding if he caught us. We respected him really, and only had a bit of fun with him, not doing anything malicious, so I hope you will enjoy these tales of an era which is long gone.

Contents

Part I

Memoirs of a Cotswold Farmer's Boy
(Or Don't Try This at Home!)

1

Early Days

I was born in 1938, just before World War II. My first recollection of life was when I was sitting in my pram being pushed by Mum in a small Cotswold village called Bladon (yes, Winston Churchill is buried there). I grew up there with my brother John, who is two years older than me, and we lived on a smallholding, where my father and mother bred chickens. One night the large building caught fire and everything either burned or was killed.

My mother was organist in Bladon church. She took me there when she practiced, and there was one particular piece of music that I loved. She played this with gusto and plenty of accelerator. The sound at full bore rattled the light fittings. It was wonderful. Sir Winston Churchill presented her with a clock in appreciation of her playing, but unfortunately she allowed us two boys to play with it, and we wrecked it. What a shame. It would have been such an heirloom.

Bladon is a pretty village, with its cottages built of that soft golden Cotswold stone which looks particularly lovely in the evening as the sun goes down. Our house was next to the entrance to the church. It used to be a laundry belonging to our family from years ago. We went to have a look at it recently and it has been converted into two upmarket houses, but they have retained the original wall running alongside the road, to keep the old appearance of it. The area is gated off, so we could not have a look round - probably just as well.

The grounds of Blenheim Palace where Sir Winston was born, and which was built by the Duke of Wellington, his ancestor, are adjacent to Bladon. Many of the men of the village used to work there, including my grandfather, who was a builder and was employed to repair the dry-stone wall which runs for miles round the grounds. One of my uncles was a local councillor, and I think that gives me the right to joke that most of them are like bananas - they start off green, turn yellow and they are never straight!

The residents of Bladon could access the grounds of Blenheim through a gate in the centre of the village, and many of us used to take a Sunday afternoon stroll down to the lake, which, by the way, was originally hand-dug, a huge task. At the end of a mile-long drive, there is a monument to the Duke, and back towards the Palace is a stone bridge over the lake. On one of the parapets, if you look closely, you will see footprints chiselled out, one of a young mother and the other of her child. Apparently times were so desperate that they committed suicide by throwing themselves into the lake. It was the first fatality in the grounds.

Not far away is Kidlington Aerodrome where my father used to work part-time to supplement his farming income. In fact, 40 years later I flew my aeroplane into the airfield, and wondered on landing whether he was there watching me making a mess of my landing. Kidlington was bombed during the war, and I hesitate to repeat my father's tales of it, because like most fathers he fantasised a bit (but not me of course).

Being brought up on a farm, we loved animals, except for a certain rooster, and I'll tell you why.

I was riding my little pedal car across the yard where the chickens and the pigs etc had free range. I don't know why, but all of a sudden he launched his attack onto my face (even in those days he didn't improve my looks). He used his beak and spurs and his wings. I think his wings were the most frightening. Apparently my face and my body was covered in blood.

My mother heard the row and rushed to me. I can still see her face, white with shock. I think the old rooster was even more surprised though, as he ended up in the cooking pot next day. By the way, I still have a scar on my forehead over 60 years later, so who really won?

We had to move from Bladon to Tetsworth, again in Oxford-shire, because we needed a larger farm. This was better than all our wildest dreams.

We could have large livestock such as cows, pigs, sheep, and, of course hens. Well, we lived quite well considering it was still wartime. We, and of course our relations, had all the milk and butter that we needed. I hated the butter. I think it would have been better if we had had such a thing as a fridge to keep it in.

In a corner of one of our fields, lived a family of gypsies who just wanted to settle down and not to go on the road again, so we said they could stay. It was mother and father and three sons, all very nice and cheerful, living in four very old wooden gypsy caravans, as you sometimes see in photos today. They taught my brother and me a good deal, such as the following:

We had some friends in the village who were hauled over the coals because their rooster woke everyone up very early in the mornings, so I mentioned this to the gypsies and they told me how to put the rooster to sleep last thing at night. I should not divulge this to you, as all England will have very quiet farmyards in the future. Well all right, here goes. First of all grab the offending rooster, hold him under your right arm, lift his right hand wing and bend his head and neck round under the wing. Then, with his head still under his wing, turn him in large circles about six times and then place him gently upon his perch, and you will see he will sleep all night. I know it's true because we have done it several times and it always works.

The local hunt was about to carry out its first meet in the area, so the gypsy lads came to see us and said, "Would you like a bit of fun with the hunt on Saturday?"

We agreed with gusto, and had a most enjoyable day. The people who rode with the hunt seemed to have no idea how to jump the fences or the gates. Some would have a go, and fly off their horses ending up either on top of the hedge or buried within it. On most occasions the horse looked horrified at the sight of the hedge, stopped dead in its tracks, and the rider disappeared over the hedge, landing flat out in the dirty wet ditch, with the horse taking the opportunity to go back home. As for the rider, well what can one say? What with being covered in mud and nettle stings and having the embarrassment of us lads with our catcalls, they staggered away as best they could. The master of the hunt waved his crop at us in a menacing way and made it all the worse for himself, as it had no effect on us. The gypsy lads had some hunting horns with them that they had made themselves - they were very clever. They dished them round, and we all split up and crawled under the hedgerows, making sure we weren't being watched. A blast on the horn, and the hunt would stop and turn and come to the sound of the horn. A few minutes later there was another blast from a horn in the opposite direction, and away went the hounds. We kept this up for some time and we thought Foxy got away this time, but as for us, we had to set to and help to repair all the fences and gates that had been demolished. Never mind, it had been good fun.

The farm was situated about two miles as the crow flies from the village school. We had to walk through the fields to get there. When it rained or there was a heavy dew, we got saturated in the long grass or the crops. There were no paths, and it was not long before our shoes rotted and fell to pieces. Money was very, very scarce. We wanted wellington boots, but clothing was rationed, and we did not have enough coupons to get them. In the end, we used to scrounge shoes and boots from very kind villagers.

There was a particular low-lying field that we walked across, and in late autumn there was a strange phenomenon with a ridge of fog from the ground to about 18 inches upwards, and about 100 yards wide. My brother used to rush into it and shout, "Look, I've lost my legs and body!" All you could see was his chest and head. We were both mystified how it came about. We also used to scour the verges along the A40 for empty Turf cigarette packets thrown away by drivers, because they included cards of football players, and we could use them for 'swaps'. It was lovely walking through the fields and looking for tracks of animals and birds. There would be moorhens and wild duck that we could distinguish, and foxes, rabbits and hares. Weasels and stoats left such small tracks it was difficult, but we often saw the animals themselves in the undergrowth.

My parents had quite a few acres of arable and sure enough, every time they planted, so the pigeons, rooks and crows would peck it up and they would have to reseed that area. My father had my brother and I stand beneath a tree before school with a shotgun to scare them off. I was standing there one day, keeping very quiet. I coughed, and there was a fluttering in the tree. I instinctively swung the shotgun up and fired, and down came a pigeon - the only thing I have ever shot in my life - including during my National Service in the army in Cyprus. That's another story for later.

On Guy Fawkes nights we would have some fun with the local village boys. We didn't have money for fireworks, so my brother John hit upon a brilliant idea and that was using bird scarers - I will explain. These bird scarers consisted of a length of slow burning rope and the bangers were sewn into the rope at intervals, so as the rope burned down slowly, the fire reached the banger and the explosions occurred one after the other. The fuses were another thing - they were so fast. We had to be quite nifty. Well, this particular Bonfire Night, we stole the bird scarer rope and pulled out all the bangers. There were about 12 in all, and when they went off the bang was magnificent, so someone had the bright idea of lighting them and quickly dropping them into a milk churn. You see, farmers had to take their milk to the main road in churns and leave them for the lorry to pick them up and take them to London. The drivers left empty churns to be used in the morning. We got to the empty churns before the farmers, and one of us took the churn lid off and the other touched the fuse with a match, dropped it in, and the lid was replaced very quickly. Then we tried to run. We only got a couple of yards when the explosion occurred. The metal churn lid disappeared in the dark and would come to earth about 30 yards away. Why we weren't killed or maimed I shall never know. The unfortunate farmer had to sterilize the churns in the morning and we heard later that the police were looking for a well-known gang from Oxford who had come down to terrorize the neighbourhood, so we got away with it!

2

Wartime

During the war, there were strict blackout rules, ie no light to show through windows, etc, no torches. Cars had their lights deflected with louvre-like strips. Imagine trying to work on the farm in the evenings, milking the cows and feeding the calves in the pitch dark. There used to be a warden who went round the village. If he saw a chink of light, he used to shout, "Put that light out," but of course we were about 2 miles from the village. My father got rather militant one evening when it was raining cats and dogs, and he lit two other lanterns, so he could walk round the cows in the yard and collect the ones who needed milking. Next morning we heard that the warden tried in vain to walk up the muddy track - when I say muddy, I mean really deep. He sank in up to his knees, struggled and fell flat on his face in the mud. He managed to get out by crawling, and of course that made things worse. He confronted my father a couple of days later and my father swore blind he knew nothing about the lights.

Another thing - we had concrete tracks put part way up the lane leading to our farm to cover up the worst of the mud churned up by vehicles. The driver of the milk lorry said,

"Good idea. I can drive up to the end of the concrete track and turn round."

Where he used to turn, there was a ditch with a small bridge over it, quite narrow. This meant every day of the year he would take several manoeuvres back and forth to turn round. That was 364 days of the year. On the 365th day (Christmas Day) he could reverse in one turn. Why? He was well lit up with beer!

Sugar was rationed in the war, just as everything else was, except bread. My father got to hear that if he kept bees he would be given 1 cwt of sugar to feed them in the winter. All my family were afraid of bees, so I can't imagine my father keeping several colonies of them. However, he went out and acquired seven or eight empty hives. He found the muddiest place in the corner of a squishy field where the cows congregated, and installed the empty hives there. He applied for the sugar from the Ministry of Food for the bees that never were.

Of course, the Ministry were suspicious as they always are, so they sent an inspector out to check on it. They sent a letter making an appointment and he duly arrived, wearing little goloshes over his town shoes, a pinstriped suit, a briefcase and a rolled up umbrella. My father said, "Certainly, come this way." The field was called '10 acre' and they had to walk diagonally across it to the corner - at least 7-800 yards. They started off OK, a bit mushy, but his goloshes could stand that. Us boys went along for the laugh - we knew what was going to happen. We got within 50 yards of the beehives. His goloshes started to become covered in a slimy, dirty, muddy mess. He stopped dead in his tracks and counted the beehives by pointing his pencil. Eventually he said, "Yes, I agree with that Mr Smith, but you are entitled to 2 cwt, as you have eight colonies." My brother and I were trying to keep a straight face, but you know at school when it is dead quiet and someone makes a funny noise and you try not to laugh; it was like that. We turned and ran back to the farm and laughed and laughed. We had never lived so well on sweet things!

We had a field that could not be combined because the gateway was narrow, between two beautiful oak trees, so my father had to get the War Agricultural Committee to hire a binder, which cuts the wheat, which then falls onto a moving canvas travelling up the machine to be made into a sheaf. Up there, when the sheaf is big enough, the mechanism pulls a string through a big needle and this in turn passes the string into a clever device called a knotter. Then the needle passes back, cuts the string and throws the sheaf out, completely bound and knotted. (Hope I'm not boring you with technology.)

Anyway, the machine arrived on our farm complete with an Irish driver/operator! We all watched him cut the first swathe and my father thought there was something wrong with the sheaves, so he bent down and found the binder had not tied and knotted them. He chased after the Irishman, got him to stop, and pointed out the fault. The Irishman looked back and exclaimed, "Sure and begorrah, she's tied a row of loose ones." My father saw the joke and collapsed in a heap, laughing.

We were about 15 miles from Benson Aerodrome as the crow flies, and one day we saw a big bomber circling in a wide arc, about 500 feet up. Liquid was coming out from underneath. We watched it as the pilot tried to put it down in the biggest field. He did a wonderful job but ploughed up the newly sown wheat into a mud bath. When they came to dismantle the plane and take it away, they did even more damage, but this was all part of the war effort! And the first time I ever tasted corned beef, because the crew gave us all a tin each. I loved it.

My family was against all cruelty to animals. They loved their cows, pigs, sheep, chickens, in fact anything that lived. Every cow had a name, the same as the cats and dogs.

During and just after the war everything was rationed so we could have just the amount of feed that the government thought the animals should have. The people who worked it out were not farmers, and they had no practical experience. The animals were hungry so we had to find other foods to supplement the rations. We mixed finely chopped hay with yesterday's milk, let it soak for a day, and then fed it to the pigs. They loved it and scoffed it down, but of course, pigs would eat anything. The cows were different. What supplement could you give a cow?

My father hit on the idea of taking the horse and cart round the village in the autumn and asking the people who had orchards if he could have either the windfall apples or the ones left on the trees. The response was wonderful, as he managed to get about four loads. He took them back to the farm, stored them in a disused loose box, did the milking and went to bed. Next morning he was mortified to find all the cows were staggering about and almost falling over. Then he saw what had caused it. The cows had broken into the loose box, had their fill of the apples, and now were as drunk as skunks!

One day on the way home from junior school, and carrying my library books, I stopped to play marbles with the local lads, despite being told always to come straight home. I suddenly realised it was late, so I picked up my marbles and ran as fast as I could uphill across the fields only to be greeted by my mother with, "Where are your library books?" So, out of breath, I about-turned and ran all the way back to get them, and then ran all the way back home again, to be greeted by my father with a cuff round the ear for being late. Was this justice or not? I wonder.

We had good laughs during the war. Whenever the sirens went off for an air attack by the enemy and the wind was either light or in the right direction, Thame's fire sirens could be heard at our farm. The dogs, three of them, used to sit in a straight line, throw their heads back, and howl uncontrollably until the sirens were switched off. The noise was appalling. We had sirens at that time because after the enemy had dropped bombs on London, they used the Home Counties as a turning point. Searchlights with long pencil beams criss-crossed the sky and when an aircraft got caught in one of these searchlights all the other lights concentrated on it and the troops opened fire. In those days it was most exciting until it became a nuisance. They never seemed to hit one, although in the daytime we saw many dogfights up high.

Of course, there was very little entertainment. There was no TV and the radio ran on accumulators. These were big acid batteries, which had to be taken to the local garage to be charged up each week. They were very heavy, so we used them sparingly, and only had the radio on for the news. There was no weather forecast, so the enemy would not know what to expect, and neither did we.

Sometimes we listened to Children's Hour presented by Uncle Mac and David. This was very comforting for children, especially those who had been sent away from the cities to live with other people, and were missing their mums and dads. The programme always ended with, "Goodnight, children - every-where." The evacuees, as they were called, found the countryside very strange after living in the cities. They did not know that milk came from cows. They thought it came from the shop.

Another programme we loved was Dick Barton, Special Agent, a quarter of an hour slot each evening in the week. Very exciting. As for the other programmes, we could not use the radio, and neither could most people.

One day we were helping my father to take the milk churns to the road for the milk lorry. We heard a commotion coming down the road. Round the bend came two little American jeeps, side by side going like stink down the main A40 road. The driver of one and the passenger of the other were fighting one another.

My father said, "Why are they fighting each other when they should be fighting the enemy?"

They disappeared into the distance, still fighting.

John and I must have seen a Tarzan film that came to our village. We watched Tarzan swinging through the trees with ease and were transfixed. If he could do it, so could we.

On our farm was a clump of elm trees about 30 foot high, so we got hold of some rope (rotten as it turned out) and tied it to a big strong bough almost at the top of a tree. We then attached more ropes of various lengths to other branches. Once that was completed, I was elected to go first, as John spun a coin he had, which always came up in his favour. I wonder why?

I climbed the tree to about halfway up, grabbed the long rope, and lined myself up to swing across to another rope. With heart thumping, I swung out and unfortunately found that my judgement was way out, so I tried to grab a branch, a rope, or anything at all.

By this time my arms were getting very tired and my hands were starting to slip down the rope. I went faster and faster until I hit the ground, which winded me, and my hands were burned pretty badly. John shouted down to me, "You did it all wrong."

I was in no fit state to answer him. I couldn't breathe because I was winded. When the pain started to go off a little, I managed to say, "If you're so ****** good, you do it."

"All right," he said, "it's easy. Watch and learn."

Grasping the rope, and with Tarzan's famous cry, he took off, and that was the time we found out the rope was rotten. It was the first time I had seen a lad trying either to fly or back pedal. He came crashing down to earth, and guess what? He was winded too. We had a lot more respect for Tarzan after that.

There was a prisoner of war camp near us, and we were allocated some workers to help the farmers. We had two at a time. They were Italian and seemed to be very nice people, especially to us young boys, as they taught us a lot, and we made them welcome at our house in the evening.

They brought a wind-up gramophone and when we wound it up, the spring broke, so my father, brother and myself stripped it down and repaired the spring, in between drinking tea and coffee, which they supplied, and Mum's apple pies.

We also had two Swiss rolls which they brought and which we had never seen before. Delicious! They brought us one each week from then on. Actually, the prisoners seemed to eat better than we did. We never did get to listen to a record, but we did eventually repair the gramophone.

We had to take them back to the camp in the blackout, with headlamps that were only 6 volt and shrouded. It looked like two glow-worms. You couldn't actually see anything. There were no streetlights or signposts - removed to confuse the enemy (and us). Even the locals got lost.

*

One day my dad went to market and bought me six tiny bantam chicks. I got the loose box ready with hay and food, and put bales of straw two blocks high all round so they could not get lost. I laid on top of these bales looking at them, as it was summer time and still light. I fell asleep and next morning when I woke up I could not make out why I was in my bed. Mum had carried me in.

We had nine cats on the farm. They all had names and Winky was the matriarch. She was incredible. She had kittens every year and her instinct was to catch rabbits for them. She would go down a rabbit hole and grab a rabbit bigger than herself, kill it, then drag it backwards to her kits about 200 yards. It took her ages, but she kept going. If she couldn't find a rabbit, she would stalk around the yard and buildings and find a rat. Rats are extremely vicious when cornered and several days she had pulled herself into the back lobby with blood pouring out of wounds and gashes. This did not stop her, because there was always a dead rat lying on the ground nearby.

One of her daughters was a bit adventurous like her, and inquisitive. She walked along the edge of a big paraffin vat storing paraffin for the tractors. She must have lost her footing because she fell in. She managed to get out and we found her writhing in pain. We could smell the paraffin, so my Mum quickly picked her up and held her under the tap - as you know, cats don't like water. After that we noticed her fur was coming out and eventually she was bald, so my mother sat down and knitted her a little coat. It had holes for her legs and her tail, and was as warm as toast. She moved about as though nothing had happened. After a few weeks my mother was changing her clothes and said, "Oh her fur is growing again." This went on until finally her fur was so silky and so long it was dragging on the floor and what a pretty cat she turned out to be.

Talking of rabbits, my brother and I were given two rabbits - one Angora and the other Blue Bevering. They did what rabbits do best and we soon had a lot more. Eventually there was no more room for extra hutches and those we had were rickety. Some rabbits escaped and ate father's young cabbage plants. He went mad and said he was going to shoot the lot when he got home that night.

My brother and I got to them first and released all the rabbits into the field in front of the house. They went in all directions and for years after we saw all different coloured wild rabbits around the area. My father said he wouldn't have shot them, but he wanted to impress on us that they should be kept under control. He gave us a whack each with a stick just to improve our memories.

My grandparents on my mother's side still lived in Bladon in a little house called Lynce View. They used to catch the bus over to the farm, mainly in the summertime, so Gramp could help with the haymaking and harvest and they stayed with us in the house for a time.

We had to skim the cream off some of the milk and make butter. To do this we had a large sweet jar, like you see in a confectionary shop. We put the cream in that and shook it back and forth on our laps. This took hours until it turned into butter. Then it had to be washed, a measure of salt added, put into butter pats or moulds to shape it, and then put into greaseproof paper. We had no electricity, consequently no fridge, so the butter was put into a meat safe, which was a metal box with perforations all round, hung up outside in the wind to keep it cool. The butter always had a rancid taste, but some people loved it.

My grandfather was as cheesed off with shaking this bottle as we were, so he thought to himself that it should be easier turning a crank. So he set to and made what was affection-ately called by us the Hurdy Gurdy. He was an extremely good workman. He made the crank out of a metal bar, and the cradle for the bottle out of a 4-bottle beer crate. He fitted the mechanism so that it shook the bottle back and forth and the two springs he planed up and made out of willow tree suckers. He assembled it onto a plinth and it worked beautifully until someone developed a commercial butter maker.

Nearly every Saturday my grandparents used to do the weekly shopping. Gramp was over 6 foot, a big-boned person and Gran was little, but quick, dressed in a black coat, hat and hatpins with white hair - very smart. They caught the bus from Bladon and journeyed to Oxford. I can remember vividly going to Gloucester Green, the bus terminus in Oxford. This place was spoken of a lot, so I remember it well. Gramp was loaded up with carrier bags, etc and off they went. They both started off together and within 50 yards of getting off the bus, Gran was nowhere to be seen. She left the order and paid for the goods in the first shop and off she darted, weaving her way through the crowds and leaving Gramp plodding along with the bags, doing a breakneck speed of half a mile per hour, picking up the goods and then off to the next shop, lolloping his way through the crowds. Gran was finished within the hour and got on the bus back to Bladon, while two hours later Gramp arrived home, to a stream of verbal abuse about being too slow. Gramp took no notice whatsoever.

He used to work on the GWR railway - the finest in the world according to him. He was the head signalman at Didcot. He used to ride his bike to the station. I thought it was Didcot and wondered how he could ride so far without lights, but I realise now it was to Long Hamborough, the nearest station, because of course he would get free travel on the train to his job.

He also smoked like a trooper. He smoked roll-ups of the strongest tobacco they had. Gran disliked it intensely and was always pitching into him about it. She did not give him pocket money, so he could not go out and buy tobacco, but she would buy him one ounce when she thought she would. When they came to help on the farm, Gramp decided that he would look around for something to mix with it to make it go further. He found some coltsfoot. He cut and dried it. When it was crisp he shredded it and mixed it with his one ounce of tobacco. The smell was atrocious - like a bonfire made of old socks and shoes, but it made him happy (and Gran unhappy).

Owing to the war effort, the Ministry of Agriculture decreed that we were to have some trees cut down and shipped off along with every farm in the area. There was some nice oak and elm.

On the Monday morning the men duly arrived with axes and cross-cut saws and their lunchboxes and flasks of tea. The trees had been marked with a white cross by an official earlier. About half way through the week, when everything was going well for them, for some reason I was off school. I thought it was fascinating and I was getting into a good rapport with the workmen. The tree started to creak and crack, so they told me to move back, which I did and saw that the tree was falling. There was a tremendous crack and the tree hit the ground. Immediately a crowd of bees poured out of the tree saying, "Who has cut our tree down?"

They saw me and made a beeline for me. I got stung about the head several times. I took off, running, with one of the woodmen slapping me about my head to get the bees off. As my mother came out of the door she saw him hit me and thought he was chastising me. She shouted, "What are you doing to my son?"

Then she saw all the bees and she took me in, slammed the door, and bathed the bumps on my head and face. Then my father said, "Oh, we'll smoke out the bees while the tree is on the ground and get the honey."

So that night he went down to the tree with paper and twigs and lit them, so he got red glowing embers and then put hay on so it smoked well. Next morning the bees had gone, so he helped himself to the honeycomb. Only one problem - the honey tasted like burnt wood. It was ruined, but we still ate it on bread and butter and for once the butter tasted good. This experience does not seem to have harmed me, as many years later I went on to become a beekeeper.

There was a very small stream in the field near the trees. My brother and I were going to do a bit of civil engineering, so we dammed the stream. The dam was about 4 foot high, made of clay. We had a lovely day getting wet and muddy.

During the night it rained and, much to my father's wrath, the water backed up and flooded the field to about 6 inches deep. We had to go and demolish the dam. This is where bird scarers came to our assistance again, because we buried a tin of them, leaving an opening. The fuses kept going off, and we retired as soon as possible. The explosion lifted the earth and clay several feet in the air and covered us in mud. A huge wall of water rose up and shot away down the stream and away. Most satisfactory.

3

The War Ends

After the war ended, my parents kept talking about lights being turned on again. Us boys didn't know what they were talking about, but we soon found out when they took us into Oxford one evening to see the lights being switched on. I was about seven years old then.

There were crowds everywhere, but it was pretty dark as usual. We wondered what lights were going to be switched on. The lights suddenly came on when we approached Magdalen (pronounced Maudlin) Bridge. They had fitted lights onto the bridge and they came on, along with all the street lights, and as we got to Carfax crossroads, all the shop lights came on. We had never seen anything like it before, everything seemed to turn golden.

Near Abingdon was a small hill. A searchlight battery stationed there turned their lights on and the beams penetrated the sky, and then they made the beams dance with each other. That was quite a display. We were mesmerised by all this, so we stopped the jeep in the middle of the crossroads, left it where it was - no one minded - and joined the crowds walking towards Gloucester Green in the centre of Oxford. People were laughing and singing. The song that was being sung a lot was "When the lights go on again all over the world." This was blasted out on loud speakers, the people joining in, singing lustily.

We walked back to the jeep eventually - and it wouldn't start. It was a bit of a worry, but a lot of men ran to our assistance and we bump started it with their help. Can you imagine anyone doing that today?

We drove down towards Gloucester Green where they had an experimental road, made of rubber blocks. It proved to be useless and dangerous. There were several accidents as soon as it rained, which it did that night. In the dry the grip was beautiful and smooth, but even the drivers of double-decker buses were renowned for getting their buses sliding, with wheels spinning. We did not have any skids that night, as we were only crawling along, due to the crowds.

It was a real party atmosphere that night. We went on with our drive, past the Martyrs Memorial and the university buildings, which were all lit up. Nobody cared what you did that night.

In the war years we could get white or red petrol. White was for general use at the full price and rationed, red petrol was for farmers' vehicles and was cheap. My father should not have been driving with red petrol for pleasure purposes. I suppose he thought the police would be fully occupied dealing with the crowds, but halfway round he must have got cold feet about it because he drove up and down the narrow streets in Oxford at quite a lick, and we all had to keep a lookout for police cars. Anyway, we made it back home without being stopped.

On the way, we passed several cars discarding their headlight deflectors, so we stopped and did the same. It made a surprisingly small difference to our lights - about one candle power. We got home and looked down the hill to the main road and for the first time we saw car lights going along the road - a sight we had never seen before.

That reminds me that a Czechoslovakian couple came to Oxford just before the war began. They became car dealers and often went up to London to get cars to sell. They gave me a week's holiday once - in Oxford. Another time they were going up to London just after the war finished and asked me if I would like to go with them. I went, but what a sight! There were bombed buildings everywhere. It was a terrible sight that I shall never forget. There was rubble still spewing out across the pavements onto the roads. Whole streets were like that. He bought a car up there, which was called an Austin Atlantic, in those days a very fast sports car. It was very good looking and that was the first time I travelled in a car doing 100 mph, taking it to a car auction in Leamington.

During the war, the farmers in our area used to take their tractors 'untaxed' down to the road and cut the grass verges, taking the hay back as feed for their animals. We did this too, and it was a cat-and-mouse game, with the police trying to catch us at it, until one day they did not turn up any more, having realised that although we were not paying for the hay, we were actually saving the Council money, by cutting the verges for them.

We did not have pneumatic tyres on the tractors, we had things called spade lugs, which was a smooth wheel with spikes sticking out of them. Some bright professor came up with a super idea, which fell at the first fence - a big steel rim bigger than the wheel, bolted on to lift the tractor and keep the spade lugs from digging into the road. Not only was it useless from conception, but useless in mud, and useless in going up an incline on tarmac, because all it did was spin - it had no grip. Just imagine what happened when we came down a slight incline with a trailer behind loaded with a ton of hay. Instead of slowing down, it speeded up, and one wheel was going forward and the other backwards, due to the type of axle, and both skidding. It was very scary. After this, we made sure we could find some pneumatic rubber tyres. These were very good on the road and on dry ground, but it still didn't stop them from skidding in the mud.

Following the end of the war, lots of army lorries and equipment had to be brought back to Army depots from abroad and around the country. One such cavalcade set off from Thame to go to Benson Airfield. The officer was map-reading and thought he could leave the road and go cross-country from Thame to the main A40 road. He thought it would be quicker! All was fine until he came to a narrow section of bridle path. It was always wet and soggy clay there.

During the Civil War between the Cavaliers and Roundheads, hundreds of years before, John Hamden had ridden down this lane, mortally wounded, and arrived at a safe house, where he died. Probably inspired by this, the officer led his cavalcade down it. Heavy armoured cars and jeeps, etc are not quite as agile as horses, and they soon became bogged down in the mud.

Spying our farm on the hill, the officer sent a soldier over to ask for help. My father readily agreed and we all went to see the fun. The old Fordson tractor did us proud. Dad drove it and did marvellously. He hardly let the wheels slip at all. He gently pulled each one and got them out. Eventually, where he reversed down to get the next vehicle, the ground became deeply rutted, so he ceased pulling and explained to the officer that he ought to have a very long tow rope of about 50 yards. With that, they went to the supply truck, dug out a tow rope about 1.5 inches thick, and about 100 yards long. That was brilliant because now he could drive onto the flat of the field where it was dry, and pull the vehicles out from there. The funny thing is, he ended up with all the rope - muddy but welcome.

Before they went on their way, they were all very grateful and they delved through their rations and we had never had so much tinned corned beef, sweetened condensed milk in cans, tea, sugar and eggs, which were gratefully received.

The rope, over the years, turned into a number of ropes of varying lengths - all very useful. One was tied to a branch high up in an oak tree, which my brother and I used as a swing. One of our friends tried it, and got it wrong. He took a run and a jump, caught hold of it and swung splat into the tree trunk.

Some of our friends came with their bikes, and we went down a little lane. It was a lovely hot day, and we all pooled our pocket money and stopped at a village shop in Moreton, a small village. We bought two bottles of Tizer, which I had never tasted before. We sat on a footbridge across a stream and had a new experience of drinking it. It was a reddish sweet fizzy drink, which would have quenched our thirst better if it had not been so warm, but we put up with it.

Another time, we took a bucket to this stream and decided to catch crayfish, which are like prawns. We had to paddle in the water to get them, as they are found under the banks. Of course, we got thoroughly soaked, but returned home proudly with a bucket full of them. Unfortunately Mum refused to cook them, because you had to throw them into boiling water, and she said she could not bring herself to do that to a living creature. I think the dogs ended up eating them.

*

If you followed this path towards Thame you came across a railway line (which alas is no longer there). We used to watch the trains go past and wave, which was quite exciting. The gates were unmanned and there was no one around to tell us how dangerous it was. We would put pennies on the line, and wait for a train to come along, usually a goods train.

We waited and waited and waited for hours and all of a sudden we heard the whistle in the distance. We hid behind the bushes and watched the train go past. When it had gone, we rushed out to pick up the pennies and see what had happened to them. They were usually flattened and twice the original size, showing how heavy the train was.

Unfortunately we were a bit too quick this time. The last carriage was the guard's van and the guard must have seen us, because next morning when we went to school, there was an official from the Railway in our assembly hall. After prayers he gave the whole school a good talking to about how silly and dangerous it is to play on the railway line. He asked if it was any of us who did this, and we said no, it was none of us - it must have been boys from the grammar school. If there was ever anything wrong we always blamed the boys from the grammar school.

Mind, sometimes we were falsely accused. An example that comes to mind concerned the son of the local butcher. In frosty weather, we used to slide across the pond near the village green. One day after school John and I had to get home quickly. The rest of the boys decided to go sliding on the pond. John and I were long gone. We heard next day that Keith Crump, the butcher's son, slid across and went through the ice. It was not very deep water, but very cold, and he ran home, saturated, and told his parents that John and Michael Smith had pushed him in. His parents contacted ours, and really had a go at them.

My mother calmly said, "But they were home early with me, because we did the milking early in order to go to the cinema." What a bit of luck, because we invariably got the blame when things went wrong.

Another time we wrongly got the blame was at school. Children went home for lunch in those days, and the lunch time was correspondingly longer, to allow walking time. John and I lived so far from the school that it was impossible to get there in the time - besides, we would have been exhausted. The school therefore allowed us to have a packed lunch in one of the classrooms. It was impressed upon us what a privilege this was, one which would be withdrawn on the slightest mis-behaviour on our part, so we were very conscious of this. The hall was used for gym on wet days, and some of the equipment was kept there, including skipping ropes.

One day, we were called into the headmistress's office and asked to account for the skipping ropes being cut in half. She believed we had done it during the lunch hour. We both vehe-mently denied doing it, but she wouldn't let it go, and made us stand to attention while she shouted in our faces. She had already found us guilty and how do you prove you are innocent?

In desperation, for some peace, I weakened and admitted it to shut her up. She then gave us the cane on the backs of our legs. That taught us a hard lesson - to find out who did it. Later someone told us it was Michael Linders who had done it. We bided our time as the matter had quietened down.

Later, several of our friends asked if they could come and play on the farm and bring Michael Linders with them. They arrived and we decided to have rides on the horse and also give each other piggy-back rides.

Nearby was a pond, waist deep, with a small island in the middle. Michael and I got on the horse and rode towards it. I said, "You get off on the island, and I will ride round and get the others and you can defend it." He was all for this, so I dropped him off - and left him there for about two hours! He couldn't get off, because the water was too deep. When we went and rescued him he said, "Why did you leave me there?"

We said, "Because you cut the skipping ropes and we got punished for it, and you never owned up."

He said, "It was only a bit of fun."

We said, "It might have been for you, but it wasn't for us."

We felt a tiny bit guilty about it, but it cleared the air, and we were friends after that.

Now comes a very sad story indeed. One day we found a baby wood pigeon that had fallen out of his nest. There was no sign of his parents, so I picked him up and took him home. I fed him on lentils etc, and called him Peep. As he grew older he became fatter and fatter, and followed us everywhere.

One cold evening we had to go out, so we looked for Peep, but he was not about. We did not worry, as there were plenty of sheds and barns where he could shelter. When we returned he was nowhere to be seen. We called and called and looked everywhere we could think of. Eventually we had to give up and go to bed. Now comes the sad bit - in the morning we found him frozen stiff in the mud - dead. Quite a few tears were shed.

Here is a more cheerful one. In our manure heap we found a nest of baby hedgehogs. Their bristles were soft, they had not become spiky yet. We fed them on mince. When we first met the parent, he rolled up into a ball, but we got him to unroll by dripping a little water on his tummy. He unrolled himself, spluttering the water away. After that, they all became very friendly and were very useful round the farm, eating up the beetles, etc.

All our hens were free range, and would nest anywhere, so we had to go out every couple of days, looking for eggs, in hedgerow, in farm machinery, in the dairy, even in the outside toilet. One day, we were looking for eggs in the hedge, when we saw some, and had to reach in to get them. John knelt down and reached in as far as he could without getting scratched and stung. He pulled out a couple of eggs, put his hand in again, and felt something warm. He pulled his hand out quickly, and the culprit was a snake!

Panic set in. John got up so quickly he got caught on brambles and stung his legs on nettles. When I looked down, the snake was heading for me. There was a little bit of wooden fence a few yards away, so I jumped up on it. Unfortunately it was rotten and it collapsed, so |I lost sight of the snake and got covered in brambles too. We had a word with Dad and described it.

He said, "It was only a grass snake. You would have known if it was an adder. It would have bitten you."

Every year at hay making time, we had two old boys, retired farm workers, long past their sell-by date, come and help us. They were pleased to make a few pounds to pay for their beer and smokes, as they called cigarettes.

They worked hard through the morning and at lunchtime they would heap up a mound of hay, sit down upon it, and open out their lunch bags. Out of them came half a loaf of bread, a large raw onion, a large chunk of cheese and a flagon of cider. Out would come their penknives and they would proceed to cut a square of bread about an inch cube, then a quarter-inch square of cheese, and pop this into their mouths, washed down with cider. They would eat the onion just like an apple. I watched them eat and drink and I remember how I would have liked to have what they were eating. My mouth watered. After their meal, they sat drinking the cider. They were no good for working in the afternoon. I think you know the reason why. They fell asleep on the hay, while the rest of us worked. Not even the sound of the tractor and other machinery would wake them.

They both had hearts of gold, and taught us boys a great deal about country life. When they did eventually wake up, around 5 pm, they would start work again until it got dark. Then Dad ran them home in the jeep.

They came to work for us in the winter time, doing hedging and ditching. That entailed cutting out the excess brambles and saplings and narrowing the size of the hedge. Then they would partially cut through the longer saplings and bend them over and interlock them with other saplings to form a strong barrier. This was called layering. It took a long time to complete, but when you looked back at what had been done, it looked wonderful, and when the spring came around, delicate green leaves grew all over their work.

With the spoil they got out, they had a bonfire every day, and at lunchtime they put some potatoes into the embers. When they were ready, they rolled them out of the fire, and dusted them off as best they could, though they still had ash stuck to them. They would cut them open and put a knob of butter and a chunk of cheese into them, and proceeded to eat them with half a loaf, of course washed down with cider. The warmth of the fire would make them drowsy, so progress in the afternoon was a bit slow. My mouth still watered, watching them eat.

The ditching was a hard, dirty job. Only spades and shovels were used, and sometimes an axe where the roots had grown into the ditch. There were no JCBs in those days. Today, machines could do the whole job in a couple of hours, instead of two men taking a week. Because of this work by them, we didn't have a flooded field. The excess water just ran away along the cleared ditch.

One day Gran and Gramp came over with a present for us boys. It was a model steam engine, about 18 inches high. It was a lovely thing, made of solid brass, which shone.

Unfortunately it did not work. Gramp felt rather guilty about that, so he set to work to repair it in the kitchen. He fired it up with coal in the fire box and water in the boiler. There were a few (!) leaks. The higher the pressure got, the fiercer and higher the leaks squirted. He released the pressure and got the soldering iron out, and proceeded, as he thought, to repair them. Actually, he made them a lot worse, or better if you like leaks. The one jet of water from the boiler was shooting up and hitting the ceiling, which had just been whitewashed. The water was horrible and black, dripping off the ceiling all over Gramp.

Gran came out and let him have it, as only Gran could. He could do nothing right for Gran. They spent their lives rowing, so it seemed to us. Gramp was placid. He just stood there and accepted it, absentmindedly still tinkering with the boiler.

After all this, he realised it wasn't the boiler's fault, but the engine mechanism, so he began to tinker with this, with Gran like a little terrier, hanging on to the back of his jacket. He dismantled all the running gear and when he came to put it back together he didn't really know where the parts went, so if they fitted somewhere near, that was good enough for Gramp. He fired up the boiler again, fully confident that the thing would work this time. Alas, loads and loads of steam, plenty of chastisement from Gran, and a faulty whistle from the engine constantly blowing and stopping, still did not turn the flywheel round.

"There you are, I told you so," said Gran. Gramp just stood there, not saying a word, puffing on a home-made cigarette, glasses completely steamed up, and his white hair turning black, along with the kitchen.

Us boys didn't care whether it worked or not. We just enjoyed the steam and the black smuts flying everywhere, and Gran trying to lay down the law and making it worse. In the end, she made him throw the whole caboodle out of the back door literally. We watched it hit the ground with an enormous explosion. The boiler had split. Now there were black smuts and sludge on the outside of the house, which had recently been painted white.

You know what happened next don't you? The terrier (Gran) came out and descended on him like a ton of bricks. She was spitting fire and brimstone, so it left him no option but to get the whitewash out and not only paint the outside of the house, but the kitchen as well. After this, the kitchen floor looked lovely and white.

Unfortunately it was supposed to be scrubbed stone. Gran came out of the living room, vibrating with anger, so then he was down on his knees scrubbing the floor. John and I felt sorry for him, so we started to help, with the result that our mops splashed the walls again, so he had to do them once more.

As he stood back to admire his handiwork, the three dogs came in from the fields, rushing through the gunge, which was still outside, and leaving muddy footprints all over his nice clean floor. The dogs were so pleased to see us, that they were jumping up, with the result that we ended up with white dogs, so they had to be washed as well (by throwing them in the pond). Gran and Gramp departed for home in silence. What a day!

Polly was a very small calf only a few weeks old. She slipped in the yard and got her front legs jammed in a grating. We managed to lift her out, but one of her front legs was bleeding, and the bone was showing. The vet was called and said, "There is no hope. She has an infection in the wound and even if she survives, she will never be the same."

That was a challenge for me, so I asked my father if I could try to get her better by putting M&B powder on it, bandaging it and keeping it scrupulously clean. He agreed, so I took my role very seriously and used hot water and Dettol and chlorous, which they used in the dairy for sterilising. I used to dress it fresh morning and evening. I dispensed with the chlorous. I was still bandaging it and using M and B powder. Polly seemed to know I was doing my best. She became so friendly when she saw me coming home from school she hobbled over to me as fast as she could and stretched her leg out for me to attend to it. It was healing up beautifully

After three months she was cured, but it didn't stop her from becoming the pet. She used to follow me everywhere and got a lot of fuss from me and an occasional handful of cow cake. She went on to produce several calves and was our best milker. Everyone was amazed, including the vet, who couldn't believe it, and of course after that I wanted to become a vet, but never did. We still have a black and white photo of Polly.

4

Teenage Years

We were growing up and getting stronger - still just as troublesome.

One afternoon I came home from school and found my father ploughing, so I went running along jumped up with him, and he let me drive the tractor. When you are ploughing you are turning the earth over with a three-furrow plough. You are going down the field and when you get to the bottom you have what is called a headland. This is used for turning purposes without the plough dug into the ground, ie lifted up. On the plough is a trip mechanism. It is worked off one of the wheels on the plough. You pull a lever and it releases a pawl, which jams the plough and lifts it. Then you quickly turn the steering wheel of the tractor to get round pretty niftily.

Well, I was driving, my father tripped the plough at the right time and everything was fine. Someone came to call on my father so he said, "Drive down to the bottom and stop and wait for me."

I agreed and he went off to speak to his visitor. While he was gone, I thought to myself, "If he can do it by himself, so can I, and he will be pleased with me if he finds I have done a few more furrows."

So I came to the end of the field. I turned round in my seat, grabbed the cord and pulled it and realised too late that I hadn't turned the steering wheel quickly enough, so the tractor and plough ended up in the ditch!

This meant we couldn't get either of them out of the ditch. It was wet soggy ground. We had a neighbour 3 miles away who had a caterpillar tractor, so I was made to eat humble pie and ask him if he could kindly tow us out of the ditch. He came along the next day with the caterpillar and, of course, he had to come across country, because a track-laying vehicle would rip up the roads. So my brother and I had to find a gate in every field we crossed, which in some cases had not been used for many years. Some were covered in brambles, so we had to cut those down with slashers, and some gates fell apart. We didn't care so long as the caterpillar got through, which it did. It took them over half a day to get to our tractor. He hooked on to our tractor and plough and pulled both out in two minutes, and there we were, finished - as we thought.

BUT we had to use the tractor plus trailer, loaded with fence posts, barbed wire, etc and go to the furthest broken gate and make up and repair that one so cattle couldn't get out, and gradually work our way to our own farm. That took a day and a half. While we were doing it, the ploughing wasn't getting done. Hence my father was in a VERY bad mood. Now that I have sons, I can understand how he felt, but at the time I thought, "What a fuss he is making."

My father bought some old railway sleepers as a job lot. He was building a lean-to shed to keep the implements dry and stop them getting rusty. He had about nine left over, so with some help from our school friends we decided we would make ourselves a raft. We got about six sleepers, braced and nailed them and launched it on the big pond.

We had hours and hours of fun pretending we were pirates etc so we decided to use the remaining three sleepers to make a motor torpedo boat. We launched that. It would only hold the weight of two lads. The big raft would hold about four. Everything was fine.

About four months down the line, the lads came to play again. Unbeknown to us, these sleepers had become water-logged. We embarked on the rafts and started chasing and avoiding. Those on the torpedo caught the big raft up and rammed it. Under it all went. There were six bodies floating in the water, coughing and spluttering.

We were yanked out by my parents. We had to be swilled down with a hosepipe and wrapped in towels while our clothes were washed and dried, and we were subjected to a severe lecture.

Talking of ponds, on a very hot day in the summer, cows were being worried and chased by the warble fly and other insects. This one cow thought she had the answer - to wade into a pond with trees on the banks. She had the right idea of dangling her tail in the water and then swishing it over her back. It kept the flies off, but unfortunately she was sinking down in the mud. She tried to move but couldn't and panicked, forcing herself deeper into the mud.

My brother found her, so he ran home to raise the alarm. We all went down to see if we could pull her out by hand, but of course, we couldn't. Her head was getting lower into the water, so my father and brother waded in and held her head up so she could breathe.

They told me to run home and get the tractor and a long rope, which I did. I returned to the pond with everything and tied the rope round the cow's horns and then over a bough, and turning right angles round the trunk of the tree, so it was pulling upwards as the tractor moved. I had to pull very slowly and gently and hold it, just taking the strain, while my father and brother were digging with their hands to clear the mud round her legs and hooves. It was a very responsible job operating the tractor of this vintage. There was no finesse about it, but we did it without hurting the cow in any way. She went off grazing as though nothing had happened, but Dad and John were really wet through and dirty, but at least nice and cool, and glad to have saved the cow's life.

During the school holidays my brother and I and two other friends pooled our pocket money and bought a balsa wood model aircraft kit. Full of excitement and expectation we worked like mad for days and days, sticking little pieces together with balsa cement, and every time we worked on it we got balsa cement on our hair and faces and everywhere else that our mother objected to. In fact she threatened to leave home twice. Eventually, we triumphantly produced the finished article.

We then decided that we would get a little jet engine for it, a grand name for a capsule of fuel that burned vigorously when lit. The capsule had a tiny hole where a special fuse went in. Then you lit it and launched the aircraft when it began to hiss. We did a couple of low level flights fairly successfully. We had to retrieve it from hedgerows and trees, but it was undamaged.

Some bright spark had the idea of launching it from the platform at the top of the windmill. In this way, it would reach its full potential. There were no hedges or trees at 30 foot, only at lower levels, so the sky was the limit. The fuse was duly inserted, four pairs of eyes full of expectancy were focused on the aircraft's smouldering fuse. It started to hiss furiously and it was launched… That was the last we saw of it ever again. We scoured the fields and hills for days, returning at night covered in scratches. We knew the general direction, but it had disappeared - probably into the Bermuda Triangle.

Talking of the windmill, it was a metal structure, not one of the romantic ones found in Chitty Chitty Bang Bang. This one was designed for pumping water out of a deep bore hole. The water was beautiful - soft and clear. After a while the council realised the water was lovely so they told us they were taking the water to supply local farms and the whole of Tetsworth. My father agreed to it, so the windmill was erected. Previously we had a hand pump, but now we had piped water. The sails made up a large 20-foot wheel with a swivelling gearbox to turn it into the wind.

One hot summer's day, our parents went on their usual grocery shopping scavenge, as we called it, and to visit friends. They went off in the jeep to Thame. After we had done the chores, my brother and I decided it would be brilliant to go and paddle in the pond. We got saturated, of course, and then there was the problem of drying our clothes.

We hit on the idea, after laying on our backs watching the sails going round, of attaching our clothes to the sails so they would dry quicker. So we wound the brake on to stop the sails, climbed up to the platform and knotted our clothes onto the steel wheel, all regularly spaced. That completed, with a sense of satisfaction, we climbed down and released the brake. Off the wheel went and the clothes were turning beautifully.

I must point out that our house was built on a hillside so anyone travelling up the A40 would see the house and windmill very plainly. Why on earth my brother and I didn't realise that on their way home our parents would be obliged to see the clothes on the windmill, I do not know, but of course they did.

All of a sudden I spotted them driving through one of the gateways off the A40, so I shouted, "They're back," and we stopped the windmill, untied the clothes and dropped them to the ground, and hurriedly got down ourselves. We dragged our clothes on willy-nilly and nonchalantly strolled towards the house.

My parents said, "What was that tied to the windmill?" (as if they didn't know).

Our eyes grew wide, "We don't know," we said innocently.

Following a few more comments from our parents, we realised the game was up. My father gave us a clip round the ear each because he said we could have fallen off the windmill or drowned in the pond. That was when I realised the pond had given us a lot of pleasure, but also a lot of pain.

One of our chores every morning at 7 am before school was to take it in turns to catch the old black carthorse called Tom, and harness him to the milk float ready to take the milk churns down to the road. We set off from the house armed with a slice of bread spread thickly with jam. In summer it was perfect, but in winter - what a different tale. Sometimes in the dark we would walk round and round searching for him without success. I would call for my brother and we covered the field in a pincer movement.

Old Tom was as crafty as a cartload of monkeys. The hedges were thick and had thinner gaps every so often. He would back into one of these and blend in with the darkness. Once we found him he would give up, but imagine his surprise when it was frosty or foggy or a heavy dew. He did the same thing, but could not understand how we found him so quickly. The secret is, we followed his footprints in the frost or damp on the ground. One up to us - four to him, and he got the bread and jam regardless.

We used to harness the sledge to Tom in snowy weather and then one of us rode him at a gallop with the other one on the sledge. The field had anthills about a foot high which froze solid, and they did cause some catastrophes. Tom loved to gallop about and kick his legs in the air and this particular time he was enjoying himself with us, when the sledge collided with an anthill and the two ropes attaching it to Tom broke and we all walked home carrying pieces of the written-off sledge. Even Tom looked dejected, with his head hung down.

One day, my brother, John, and I were bored to tears. On the farm we had some old wooden beer crates, and as we lived on a hill, we decided to make a buggy, or go-cart. We found some old pram wheels joined by axles. I have no idea where they came from - perhaps some occupants of the house who lived there before us.

At any rate, my brother took it upon himself to make this contraption - he knew it all! The rear axle had to be joined to the wooden beer crate. This was quite a challenge. We had some nails 6 inches long. He banged these nails through the wood part-way and then bent them and formed them round the axle, which was metal. So there were about 12 nails used for that. We both thought. "Oh, that is good enough," so then came the draw bar, a long piece of wood about 6 foot long. That was nailed underneath the box and protruded forward, so now we had to work out our steering.

We mounted the front axle onto another piece of wood. It had to be fixed to the long draw bar, so that it could swivel right and left, enabling us to steer. We did this by passing a 6-inch coach bolt through the axle, then through a spacer, and then through the draw bar, and we screwed a nut on the end to hold it securely. We then tied a piece of rope on the outer edges of the axle to steer it, rather like reins on a horse.

Now came The Trial. With great pride and quite a bit of trepidation, my brother sat in the wooden box, or cockpit as we called it. He took hold of the steering rope and I gently pushed him down the slope. This was successful, so we became more daring, and we dragged the go-cart up to a higher level. My brother again sat in and steered. The contraption hurtled down the bank and travelled a good 150 yards, coming to a stop on the level ground. So far so good.

I said, "Can I have a go now?"

"Yes," he said, "as long as you pull it up to the top, and I will give you a push down."

So we started manoeuvring it up the steep bank. I had the rope round my shoulders to make it easier, so I could use my hands to climb up on all fours. Well, I slipped over on the slippery grass, and was lying face down. John was still pushing hard, and I suppose the contraption bounced up in the air at the front and then crashed down on the back of my leg. I felt a searing pain.

I was screaming and crying and John lifted the contraption off me, but left the rope round my shoulders. Next thing I knew, I was being catapulted upwards, and then rolled until I reached the bottom of the hill, with the contraption nearly strangling me with its rope. John came running down and he was more concerned with whether the contraption was broken, than with my terrible injuries. I was in agony and he casually said, "Oh you're bleeding," so I swivelled over onto my side and looked down at my calf muscle and notice a spurt of blood every time my heart beat. We both looked at this interesting phenomenon, fascinated.

I don't know how my father arrived on the scene so quickly. It may have been the screams, or perhaps the crashing noise, but he released me from the rope and used it as a tourniquet, that is, he tied it tightly round my leg above the wound, to stop the bleeding. Then he turned the contraption over onto its back and there, sticking out about 2 inches, was, to our amazement, one of the 6-inch nails, covered in my blood.

My mother insisted that my father took me to the doctor's surgery, and I was given a tetanus injection, which hurt more than the 6-inch nail. After that, my leg became very painful and stiff, so any of the chores we had to do were transferred to John, because I could only hop. For quite a while, I took advantage of this and poor John was overworked.

What happened to the go-cart? It was destroyed and, I think, burned. I was still hopping for what seemed months, but one day I was on my own and walking normally, until John saw me, and that was the end of my convalescence, but I had the scar for years. It is still there - rather faint now - but I charge 50 pence to look at it. Please bring a magnifying glass! Funny, only the girls want to see it - morbid lot - the boys couldn't care less.

One day, John and I did something we never normally did - we left a gate open, and the cows got into the wheat, and trampled it. Our father went absolutely berserk. We were quite frightened.

He shouted, "If I catch you, I'll give you both a good hiding."

Well, we knew the signs, so we took off. There was one tree that my father could not climb. It was in the middle of a field, so we made a beeline for it, and about 100 yards behind was our father, running as fast as he could. We reached the tree and shinned up it in double-quick time.

At this point he gave up and proceeded to get up onto the tractor and plough, and started ploughing the same field. This was early morning on a very hot day. Of course, we became hot and thirsty, but he went on ploughing. We thought we would creep down the tree while he was concentrating on the ploughing. He would craftily wait until we were within jumping distance of the ground, and then he would quickly stop the tractor and run like a demon towards us. We had to shin back up again, twice as hot and twice as thirsty. This went on till well after lunch would have been, when our mother came out and told our father off, good and proper, because we were getting sunburnt. My father had a short fuse in those days, probably shortened by having to bring us two boys up.

Another time, Father decided to have the cowshed concrete floor renovated, so he got some men in to do it. They arrived with their cement mixer, which was driven by a single cylinder diesel engine. When they went home that night, John and I decided, in the interests of our education, to find out how it worked. We managed to start it, after pulling levers and pressing rods, and my brother said, "It's just like a roundabout at the fair. Would you like a ride?"

At the time it sounded good, so the engine was stopped and I climbed into the mixer. John proceeded to start the engine and away we, or I went. Of course, I began to feel sick, and my rotten brother found out that if he moved this lever, it made the engine speed up and the barrel went round faster. I pleaded with him to stop, but he carried on until I started crying and bawling. It seemed to take ages to slow down, so when it did stop, he turned the wheel on the end of the mixer, which tips the barrel on its side. Out I slithered, banging my head on the ground and still howling and protesting. I managed to stand up, but was staggering about bumping into everything and making a fool of myself. Isn't it horrible, when you feel rotten and someone is laughing uncontrollably?

My father had a metal scrap heap, where he used to throw broken mower parts etc and old 5-gallon petrol drums. Those drums had been on the scrap heap for years and years, with their lids off, steadily rusting away.

DON'T DO THIS AT HOME!

Like a twit, I had acquired some matches this day, and had nothing to do immediately. I was passing the scrap heap, noticed one of the petrol drums, and wondered what was at the bottom of this particular one.

It was dark inside of course, so I lit the match and dropped it into the empty drum, and then looked down into it from the top, and all of a sudden there was a W H O O S H! and my eyebrows and lashes had gone, plus all the front of my hair. I didn't care much for my hair anyway, because it was dead straight, and wouldn't lie down, but stood bolt upright. Although the pain was severe on my face and it turned bright red, by treating it with creams etc, after about six months it got better, and my hair also grew, but now the front was wavy, and it is still so today (what's left).

During harvest time, we were all expected to help. This particular day we were using a binder (you remember what that is) and I was walking behind it and as the corn was cut, it left stubble behind. Low down was a mouse's nest, with five little mice in it. Being soppy over animals at that time (and now) I picked them all up and put them in the pocket of my jacket and carried on working. When I got home, I noticed that the farm cats were taking a great interest in me, and I suddenly realised why - I put my hand in my pocket to where I had put the mice - not one of them was in there, but there was a hole leading into the coat lining.

My mother went mad, because the mice would ruin my jacket and indeed they were running about between the lining and the outer fabric. I was told to go back to where I got them from and let them out. Have you ever tried showing a wild animal what to do? I got them near the entrance of my pocket, expecting them to jump out, but they must have caught sight of my face and decided to stay inside. There were five of them, all running in different directions. Two of them took umbrage at my hand feeling for them, and they latched onto me with their teeth, so I pulled them out, still attached to me. Although I was bleeding quite a bit from the bites, I never got angry with them, because I loved animals. Then I had to pinch their little toes gently to get them to release their grip As soon as they reached the ground they were off.

Two gone, three to go, so I thought, "Well, they didn't really hurt, so here goes again," and managed to get all three in one corner. Only one latched on this time, and he was soon whisked out. Then it was a free-for-all to get the other two. Just at that moment, one of our inquisitive dogs came over to me. This made everything worse, because the dog could smell the mice and the mice could smell the dog. The mice rushed round and round, the dog was burying his nose in the fabric and I was piggy-in-the-middle.

Mother saw what was happening, and called the dog away, and giving me a pair of scissors, told me to cut the lining. The two mice fled into the field, but it did stop me from picking up little mice again.

The trouble with being bored was boredom and no money, like the time we got into the Tetsworth church one night just as a 'dare'. Churches were not locked in those days. We climbed the steps to the first floor where the bell ropes came down from the bells and continued through holes cut in the floor, so the bell-ringers stood on the ground floor, down below to ring the bells. This was on a Saturday night. One of our group had a little Ever Ready torch, as much use as a glow worm. Be that as it may, we managed to pull the bell ropes back through the holes and tie them off about 20 foot from the floor. Then we removed the stepladder and hid them - a bit mean I know, but we didn't do any damage.

Mr Plod the policeman was called in. He conducted his own enquiries and came to a great discovery and that was he didn't know who did it. Next morning, Sunday, was very quiet. The bells had fallen silent and we all slept on peacefully.

Mr Plod had a smashing quiet life generally. There was almost no crime, so he devoted himself to chastising us youngsters. There was a love-hate relationship between us.

Apple scrumping caused a laugh. You see, what happened was, he would get a phone call saying there were lads stealing apples in this orchard. Down he would ride on the 'county camel' bike. One of us would stand in the undergrowth, ie stinging nettles and brambles, making sure there was a way of escape. The rest of the guys ducked down behind the fence. When Mr Plod saw the decoy, he would clamber over the fence, shouting, "Stay where you are." The decoy was munching an apple and pretending not to hear. With his eyes on the decoy, Mr Plod would jump down off the fence, straight into these long brambles and stingers. There he was stuck, as the ground was lower on that side of the fence. The rest of us had a free-for-all, stuffing our shirts with apples. However, it was a wasted evening because the apples turned out to be cookers, and too sour to eat. So who won really?

There were strict licensing laws for public houses and one of Mr Plod's duties was to cycle from his home, a mile away, and go round all the pubs making sure they were closed at 10 pm. He was very strict about this and woe betide any pub that was still open. This gave us another opportunity to torment him.

He would cycle very slowly and ponderously from his house a mile away, dismount from his cycle (or county camel), laboriously pull his watch out of his pocket and note the time. He leant his bike against the pub wall and at precisely ten o'clock he would walk into the pub and check what was going on. Of course, there were several pubs in Tetsworth, so his bike was important, and he would ride it to each pub in turn, following the same procedure.

Us lads laid in wait until he leant his bike against the wall of the first pub, and went inside. Then we crept out, quietly took hold of the bike and wheeled it round the corner, out of sight. Then one of us rode it and the rest followed him on their bikes back to Mr Plod's house. There, we leant it against his house. Then we returned to the village, where there was a commotion going on both inside and outside the pub. He was going to jail everyone. He was sure they were all guilty, and his suspicions fell mainly upon the heavy drinkers. They retaliated by saying that he had been drinking himself, and had forgotten to bring his bike. We lurked round the corner, laughing and laughing. The drinkers in the last pub came off best as they had the longest drinking time they had ever had before. Of course, when he got home, there was his bike, and he wasn't sure whether he had taken it or not!

When we got home, we told our father, and he laughed and said it reminded him of something his father had told him about. An old man in his village used to go by horse and cart to his local pub, where he proceeded to drink too much, every time. His friends used to turn the horse and cart round, lift him into it, and the horse knew the way home, and took him straight there by itself. On one occasion, they decided to play a trick on him, and they turned the horse around in the shafts, so it was facing the cart, in other words, the horse had to push the cart. They put the old man in the cart, and set the horse off for home. Of course, the horse was thoroughly confused. At the first gateway it came to, it missed and the cart ended up in the ditch, where it stayed until the morning.

Mr Plod lived on the outskirts of the village and one night, we drove a stake into the lawn, right outside his front door. Then we got a stout rope, tied it to his door handle and then onto the stake. Then we made our way to the phone box, rang him up, and said, "Someone has fallen into the ditch by the Hope's farm."

We watched from a distance and were shocked when he appeared from the BACK of the house, wheeling his trusty steed. We didn't expect this, because he had to walk past the stake and the rope. When he saw it then it dawned on him that it was all a hoax. The funny thing is, he always came out of his front door. He knew at once who had done it. Over the next week, he singled us out one by one, and he would give each of us a darn good hiding. Our bottoms were really sore. When we got home, we had trouble sitting down. My father inquired why we were fidgeting and suddenly realised what had happened, and gave us another good hiding for torment-ing the policeman. We thought twice about doing it again for a while, but soon went back to our practice of including him in all our fun.

I often think of my mother's kitchen and wonder how she managed with all the mess we made. There were no microwave ovens, no dishwashers, no fridges, and no washing machines - in fact, no electricity.

The washing was done in a copper. This was a square, brick-built structure with a large copper container in the top complete with wooden lid. At the bottom of the structure, there was a square hole where the fire was lit. When the water in the copper became hot, the washing was put in with washing powder, and brought to the boil. When it was clean, it was fished out with tongs, rinsed in a bowl, and the water was squeezed out in a mangle.

The mangle had two rollers and the clothes were inserted between them, and a handle on the side was turned to make the clothes pass through. There were no tumble driers, so everything was hung outside on the line to dry, and was ironed later on, by an iron which was heated on the fire, as we had no electricity. On frosty Mondays the washing went stiff, and overalls that we brought in were stood in the corner to melt and gradually sink to the floor. It took all day to do the washing, and everybody kept out of the way of their mothers, as they were very snappy and irritable.

We had a kitchen range. This was a fire which was always alight and had an oven one side for cooking and a smaller one the other side for bread. It was black, and our job on Saturdays was to polish it with blacklead polish. It used to stand on red bricks, which had to be restained each week with Cardinal Red. For some years, Mother cooked on a so-called 'modern' stove, heated by paraffin. Everything reeked of paraffin, food, kitchen, everything. Then one day she had a Calor Gas cooker - the latest thing, which looked like today's cookers, but with a Calor Gas cylinder beside it. The trouble was the gas did not last long and had a habit of running out when a cake or dinner was half cooked. Another reason to leave the kitchen quickly!

We had three dogs, and my father complained bitterly at the cost of feeding them. We used to fill them up with a couple of loaves, soaked in gravy, but he still grumbled. One day, when our grandfather was staying, he said, "Well, there's plenty of wheat. I've got an idea."

He got a pile of wheat, crushed it with a rolling pin, put it in a dish with some water, and put it in the paraffin stove. The dogs were ravenous, but even so they turned their noses up at it at first, but eventually hunger got the better of them, and they ate it. The noise of it cracking between their teeth was deafening, with three of them, and we couldn't stand it. So there was another idea that 'bit' the dust.

They were two labradors, Bill and Bess, and a bull-mastiff, Duchess. We don't know if the labradors were natural hunters, but because they were hungry, they certainly came back with rabbits, etc. The bull mastiff used to chase anything that rolled, eg a ball, a wheel, etc. When we were ploughing the fields, she would go to the back of the plough, where there was a single wheel which adjusted the depth of the furrow. She would go up to the metal wheel and try to stop it, barking at it. Even when we ploughed a 5-acre field in one day, she chased it all day, until we could do no more. She must have been exhausted and covered in mud, but next morning she was ready for another session. We think she thought she was on the payroll.

During the winter evenings, the three dogs were allowed into the lounge where the fire was. They plonked themselves down in front of it, stopping us humans from feeling any warmth. They were very big dogs, and if they laid down there was not room for them all, and there was a fight, so they used to sit bolt upright in a row. The old mastiff, after a little while, began to nod off to sleep. She was in the middle. The family knew what was coming and sat and watched. Her head dropped lower and lower until her nose touched the hot grate. Her head jerked up again and then began slowly to drop again as she fell asleep. We all thought she was a bit thick as it happened time and time again. But she was a good dog, and was a real heroine once, and this is how it happened…

We used to let the cows roam with the bull. One day Mother went to round up the cows for milking, which she did every day. This time she went to round them up and the Ayrshire bull, unknown to her, was in a bad mood. He lowered his head and charged at her, knocking her down. She was screaming, and the dogs heard her. The bull was knocking Mother about on the ground with his horns. Mother thought it was the end of her. She was resigned to the final charge and goring by the bull, when all of a sudden she noticed he had left her alone. She heard the dogs yapping, so she looked round and there were the labradors dancing round the bull, barking, while the mastiff, a very heavy dog, was swinging from the bull's ear, which she had clamped onto. It must have hurt the bull, because his bellow changed into a blood-curdling cry of pain.

By this time, my brother was alerted to it all, and saw what was happening. He rushed and got the gun. He was going to shoot the bull, but Mother pleaded with him not to, although she was badly bruised all over. Then my brother and I carried her home, while the dog was still firmly latched onto the bull.

Dad didn't know what was going on, because he was in the milking parlour, preparing the milking machine, which was noisy. I rushed to tell Dad and took over the milking, so he could go and nurse Mum.

The bull didn't do himself any good at all over that. We got two 56 lb weights that were used for weighing sacks of corn, and attached one to each end of a steel rope. Then we got another rope, attached it to the ring in his nose and tied it to the steel rope, so it could move up and down and give him quite a bit of movement. Never again was he allowed to go free, as he was unreliable and we could not trust him.

Mum eventually got better. She was confined to bed for quite a time and yours truly had to do the cooking! Never was a family so glad to see anyone recover. They were heartily sick of eating the same menu every day. Of course, food was rationed. I could do potatoes and sprouts and keep heating up the tiny joint day after day, and for a treat we had split and burnt sausages. Dessert every day was Cremola, a kind of custard in a tin. No wonder Mum made a miraculous recovery. As for the bull's ear, the mastiff had shredded it, and he went around with one ear looking like a rubber glove, and he was very respectful toward the mastiff.

5

Careers

Working on the farm was fine in the summer. We loved being out in the fields, but for most of the year it was cold and wet. For instance, in the winter, we had to cut kale for the cows. Kale is a kind of cabbage that cows like. It grows about 5 foot (almost 2 meters) high with great big leaves. In wet or dewy weather, the leaves would get full of water. We had to bend down to cut the main stalk as low as possible, so as not to waste any. Of course, as we chopped into the stem we got showered with ice-cold water. In those days we had no effective waterproof clothing, and why we didn't get pneumonia I don't know. There was only one worse job - on a freezing day it was ice showering down, but it still had to be done.

My teenage years were, to say the least, hard work from the start. We had jobs to do before school and then when we came home we were expected to help with the milking of the cows, Polly included. If not milking them, it was grinding oats for the cows to eat when being milked. This began with starting the tractor. You see, there were no electrics such as a self-starter, so one had to crank it over by hand with a starting handle inserted at the front. In cold weather you froze and in hot weather you sweated.

Let me go through the starting procedure with you. We had to start the tractor on petrol, which was in a separate tank on the tractor. When the engine had started, it was left to warm up for about five minutes. Then you turned off the petrol tap and turned on the TVO tap (a form of paraffin). Then the engine ran smoothly and one could drive it to whatever task was required. Having done all this, we were ready to do the grinding of the oats.

I drove into the muddy yard, which was dreadful when it was raining, because unlike today's tractors with heaters, air conditioning, radio and CD players, sprung seats and cabs and a windscreen wiper, in the past there were no such luxuries. Be that as it may, even in the rain you had to keep going and line the tractor up with the mill. You did this by eyeing both pulleys up as straight as possible. As it was dark, a lantern was placed on the mill pulley and you could just about see the tractor pulley, because you were close to it. Then it was time to fit the drive belt between the two of them, tension the belt and select the pulley gear, slowly letting out the clutch. Then you set the correct revs. Dismounting from the tractor, you went into the dry shed and filled the hopper with oats and milling began, in other words, crushing.

If the drive belt managed to stay on all through it was a miracle, but in the wet, if it came off once, it came off dozens of times, right into slimy mud. There was no way of cleaning it or drying it, so you stuck it on and hoped it would stay, so back onto the tractor, select the gear, and let the clutch out even slower than before, allowing centrifugal force to displace the mud etc, and remember where one was watching the pulleys? You guessed it - right in the firing line of the mud!

*

As we grew older we had to think what career to go in for. We had both had enough of farming and were fascinated with engines and how they worked, so, he being older than me, John found a job at the Aylesbury Motor Company Ltd, working on the older Ford cars and the very revolutionary Mark I Consuls, Zephyrs and Zodiacs.

I left school a year later and landed a job with a firm called R and E Potter Ltd in my home town of Thame. They were agricultural engineers and I made good use of my time there. I had a flair for welding and the foreman noticed and told the bosses, so they in turn sent me to evening classes at an agricultural college, where I learned all the techniques of welding and how all metals were either cast or manufactured. After this, my firm made me the firm's welder. There was no such thing as Mig and Tig welders, but gas and arc.

Dealing with farmers was very challenging. Things that broke on the farm were bodged up with either baling wire or baling twine. They didn't like to pay very much, so they came to me and said, "Smother a bit of weld on here, boy, and I'll give you half a crown."

This was not on in two ways. One, I was brought up not to lie or to steal, and this would have been stealing, and two, I loved my job, so I didn't even start. If I had taken the money I would have made a small fortune. I got on so well with welding in the works and I'd passed my driving test, so the firm bought me an Austin A40 pick-up truck. I loved this because it was modern and, of course, it had independent front suspension. When the shock absorbers wore and got weak, I used to pull up sharply to impress the girls, because when I came to a stop, the truck sat there and gave a couple of small bounces. I don't know why, but it did.

Equipped with my new A40 pick-up, I fitted it out for gas

welding and arc. Two very large gas cylinders were chained to some brackets I made up. The arc welder was on small metal wheels, so I screwed a piece of wood to the floor near to the front of the truck bed and this acted as 'chocks'. Loaded with all the necessary welding rods and some matches, my first farm call came in. All excited, I set off in my new truck. We reached the farm and were met by the farmer at the gate.

"Through here, boy," he shouted.

To my dismay, his yard was full of cows, excrement and soggy straw. My poor shiny truck!

I had to do as he said, after all he was paying the bill. He directed me over to a covered barn and there in the corner was an electric motor that was driving a pulley shaft on the next floor up. The main bearing housing had split and the farmer came out with the usual thing: "Smother a bit of weld on that, boy. Won't take you two minutes."

I had to protest for two reasons. One, the bracket had to come off the shaft, and two, if I had used the welding plant, the whole building would have gone up in flames, because there was a lot of dry hay and straw strewn about everywhere. So I refused to do it unless I took the bearing off.

The farmer was very agitated about this and said I didn't know what I was doing, I was useless, and I was trying to force the price up. It was no good trying to explain to him.

"I'm going to telephone your gaffer, boy," he said, so with that I reversed out of the yard, only to get stuck in a rut. That was embarrassing. I did not want to ask him to tow me out with his tractor, so I found some old bits of wood and gravel, and put it under the wheel that was skidding. He chuckled to see me stuck, and it made me more determined to get out by myself. I did this by slipping the clutch a lot, and very little revs, and just crawled out. His face dropped.

Then he said, "Your gaffer is coming out to see what a mess you have made of everything."

I said, "Good." Sure enough, the foreman came out just as I drove out of the yard. He told me to stay in the van and that he knew this farmer of old. He confirmed what I had said to the farmer about the fire hazard. He even told the farmer to remove all the straw and chaff over and around the electric motor. I omitted to say that the building was of old dry wood. One spark and it would have gone up.

It needed two fellows to remove the shaft and pulleys, which had been up there for donkey's years. They were put on a lorry and brought back to the works for me to make the necessary repairs. He did not even thank me or say goodbye after the job was completed.

In the early days of my apprenticeship, I had to cycle to work across fields and a muddy overgrown lane. During the summer I got my face scratched with brambles, but put up with it because at least it was summer and I could ride the bike. However, during the winter it was ride, push and carry the bike in all weathers. Mud used to collect between the wheel and the forks, and it became impossible to push.

One very dark night whilst carrying the bike, I had to climb over a wooden fence, which was joined onto a tree, and the trunk was part of the fence. This particular night, pitch black, no street lights anywhere, I felt my way to where I thought the fence would be, found myself about 5 yards out, and groped for the fence. I always climbed over by the tree, because the ground was dry, with no mud, and I could lift the bike over by leaning on the fence and not get snagged by barbed wire. Anyway, I digress. As I leant over, something hit me on the back so hard I thought Lucifer had come for me. I was scared to death, and to my amazement it turned out to be one of our cats, so not only was I carrying the bike on my shoulders, but the cat as well. He curled round my neck and it was lovely and warm, so I didn't mind giving him a lift.

Sometimes, if I was early I used to cycle the main road way, and if a slow-moving lorry overtook me I used to take hold of the tailboard and get a free ride. Everything was fine. I used to keep my eye open for the police. The lorry speeded up when it was going downhill, obviously, and at a particular hill, at the bottom I would have to turn left. Sure enough, the lorry speeded up and when he came to the intersection, he braked very hard, looking for his way, so consequently this propelled me forward in a straight line, but I wanted to turn left. You know on a bike, when you want to turn left, you don't just turn the handlebars, you lean over. By this time I had a nice head of speed, tried to lean, but I went diagonally onto the grass verge, jumped a ditch, and then crashed into brambles and stinging nettles. The driver of the lorry was oblivious to all this, so I had to get myself out of it.

First of all, the front wheel was buckled, the saddle bag was missing, my lunch bag was floating in the ditch, and I was being stung and scratched all over. I managed to get out after some time, so instead of being early for work, I was late, and got a rollicking, despite putting on an Oscar-deserving display of broken arms, damaged legs, ripped clothes, and dazed state. The foreman just brushed it aside and continued with his lecture.

Following my stint at evening classes on welding at the Rycotewood Agricultural college, I did quite well, so my parents decided to pay for me to attend full time to do an engineering course. The college was called the Rycotewood College of

Engineering and Rural Crafts. That included carpentry, black-smithing and welding, and agricultural engineering. This meant boarding in at the college. One advantage I had was that home was only 6 miles away, so I could pop home at the end of the day and be back before 10.30 pm.

My fellow students came from all over the country, and tried to be friends with me for two reasons. One, I rode a motorbike and two, they liked to come home with me and have a good meal. I think I took everyone in turn home during my time there.

My firm was very good, as while I was on the course they kept me on and paid me £1.10s.0d (that is £1.50 in today's money). It wasn't wonderful, but they needed me and I was very grateful. Normally I earned just over £2, which I had to give to my mother in its unopened envelope. I was lucky if she gave me a little back, but she needed the money for my keep, and to be fair, if I needed parts for the motorbike, she paid for them, and I also had free petrol.

Whilst at Rycotewood I found out how acetylene gas was made, which the college already made itself, using a generator. The process entailed having a vat of water in a sealed container below a hopper of carbide crystals. These crystals were regulated to fall into the water below. Carbide and water react, giving off acetylene gas. This was pumped into a pressurised vessel to be used in blow torches. We lads thought, "What a good idea for a bit of fun."

We could go to the metal store and in there were kept the bags of carbide, so, craftily, we used to grab a handful and nonchalantly walk into the blacksmiths' shop, where they had five forges, each with its own trough of water. The blacksmiths had their fires blazing away and were watching their metal heating up and were unaware of our presence. We quickly dropped the carbide into the troughs and moved away as quickly as possible. There was a huge big flame, orange and red, followed by a loud W H O O F! and a lot of black smoke. The blacksmiths looked bewildered and staggered out of the smoke and all of us students were behind the wall laughing our heads off. I think that everyone must have done this over the years, because we noticed it turned the water white and there was quite a lot of white sediment built up at the bottom of the troughs.

My tutor noticed that I had a natural aptitude for gas welding and electric arc welding. He encouraged me to read books about metal grain structures, and then he would test me in practice. It was very good of him, because occasionally he would come in during the evening and put me through my paces.

One evening, he dropped a bombshell, by saying he had entered me for the BOC welding competition, which was held in a big marquee in a big city showground. This time it was in Cambridge. We had to travel there by train, which was quite exciting. We got to the showground, found the marquee, and went inside. There were other young lads there with their tutors. I looked at them all, and thought, "I stand no chance." However, all the equipment was laid out on the benches, together with the test pieces. There were fillet welds, and buck welds in mild steel. Then we came to the more difficult aluminium welding and cast iron. Flat on the bench, it was a doddle. Then it was quite sneaky. Things were suspended above our heads and we had to weld vertically, which was extremely difficult because with aluminium one could not see when it was going to melt. If you were not careful, all you got was a pile of molten aluminium in a blob on the bench and probably down your clothes and in your shoes. Cast iron was my speciality, so I romped through that, and I found that I had finished all my projects and asked my tutor if I could go and look round the showground.

He agreed, but said, "Be back in an hour and a half."

So off I went, looking round all the new machinery and eyeing up all the girls. I forgot about the time. Instead of an hour and a half, I had two hours. I had to leg it back to the marquee, where I expected to meet a very angry tutor, but no. He was all smiles, and congratulated me on becoming Champion of England for welding!

BOC offered me a job demonstrating their equipment. At that time I said I would think it over and let them know, but of course when we moved I felt it was my duty to help my father in the new garage. More of that later. As for the championship, I thought I was going to have the big silver cup, but no chance. Rycotewood College laid claim to it! All I got was a cheer at assembly next morning, and then back to work.

That November 5th, we were given permission to have a bonfire and fireworks. The woodworking chippies were given old pianos by the public to provide wood for their classes, because all wood was rationed. We pushed one of the pianos nearer the bonfire and all the students gathered round for a sing-song. Well, a friend of mine and I pre-arranged to open the lid of the piano and discreetly drop two lit bird scarer bangers into it. The pianist had just got into the swing of it and was letting rip. Next thing he knew, the piano had disappeared and he was strumming the air, surrounded by a pile of splintered wood, and students laughing their heads off. Thank goodness there was no health and safety in those days!

That same evening we commandeered a combine harvester. We waited until all the tutors were in the Common Room drinking coffee, to warm themselves up at the end of the evening. Then we pushed the combine down to the main gate, which had quite a narrow archway and was easy to block. We jacked the combine up and took the wheels off. We rolled them down the sloping lawn into Rycotewood lake, and some bright spark suggested we stuff potatoes up the tutors' car exhausts. You can imagine what happened when the tutors came out and tried to start their cars. The exhausts split and made a dickens of a noise. Meanwhile, some wag climbed up onto the college roof and put a gazunder (potty) on top of the weather vane.

We all went to bed very merry, only to be woken up by the irate tutors and ordered to wade into the lake and retrieve the wheels. You can imagine how cold that was on a frosty November night. They knew I was the instigator - I always got the blame, I don't know why - so the furthest wheel was assigned to me. I had to swim out to it and when that job was completed and all the wheels were replaced, they opened up the workshops and the blacksmiths' shop and made us repair and renew the car exhausts. When the job was eventually completed it was too late to go to bed, and we applied ourselves to the day's work in a zombie-like state, with students dozing off over their written work in the classrooms.

In the machine shop there was a sliding door between the actual workshop and the cloakroom. We had a tutor called Inky Stephens. He had an obsession, so we thought, with keeping doors closed, because every student who came through the sliding door left it wide open. It made him very bad tempered, so he kept on saying, "I will invent something to close the door and cut your feet off at the same time."

Two or three of us had the idea that if we could make the door close with a spring it would make him better tempered.

We thought out a pulley system, so when the door was opened a weight was lifted, and when you let go of the door it should close slowly and gently, but firmly as the weight came down. Unfortunately we did not get the right weight to close it gently. It was too heavy, and then we ran out of time in our lesson to test it and get it right. We were the last class that day.

Next morning we went to Assembly and Inky was nowhere to be seen. Funny. We were sent to our classes. Inky was still nowhere to be seen. Next thing, Matron came bustling in, breathing fire and brimstone, saying, "You have put Mr Stephens into hospital."

The door had slammed on his leg very fast. He did not have time to get out of the way before it slammed into his leg. Actually the leg was not broken, only badly bruised.

We thought we would all get a severe telling off, or be kept in, or even asked to leave, but he re-appeared, beaming across his face and said, "Thank goodness you've got a bit of gumption to work out a problem for me, though very heavy handed. Let's work out the formula you should have used, shall we?"

That was worse than a detention! However, the mechanism was there for years afterwards.

Every so often the college put on a party and invited the local girls, so we could have some dancing. There was a group of us who just went for the grub, which we devoured in double-quick time. As for dancing, what a sissy thing to do. Our group thought the girls were useless, but the principal rounded us up, determined to civilize us, and we had to get tidied up, looking like Little Lord Fauntleroys, and stay for the rest of the evening at the party, watching the girls dance with the boys who could dance.

We took the mickey out of the boys with catcalls, but the sting in the tail was that at the end of the evening the principal lined all us boys up and the girls had to link arms with a boy each and be escorted through the streets of Thame to their homes. We didn't think much of that.

There was absolutely no conversation between the girl on my arm and myself, and apparently the rest of them were the same BUT we had a lovely write-up in the local paper, the Thame Gazette (or the Thame Guts Ache as we called it) saying how we were being brought up to be perfect gentlemen. How wrong they were! After we deposited the girls we ran as fast as we could back to the college. The dances didn't cease, but we always had some pressing engagement - AFTER we had eaten the food.

The Thame cinema used to show films twice a week. The cinema was just a big room with a floor sloping down toward the screen. It was not posh like today's cinemas. The seats were just benches. It wasn't that the films were good, but there was no entertainment - no TV. They used to have a lovey-dovey film accompanied by whistling and catcalls from us boys, until the usherette came down and blinded us with her torch and threatened to send us out. Sometimes the film would break down and usually we would start singing "Why are we waiting?"

The students who came to the cinema were from all over the country and they had different accents. Uproar occurred when the film suddenly stopped. It went pitch black, and a North Country voice shouted, "Ee, light t'candle, lad."

At the end they always played the National Anthem and we had to stand to attention and woe betide us if we didn't. The benches we sat on were each side of the centre aisle, free standing, so when the Anthem was over we were supposed to file out in an orderly manner. We did - up to a point - because a couple of us who were last out always managed to knock down the last bench, which then clattered into the one below, causing a domino effect, right down to the last one. We thought it was very funny and no one else had done it before, but the proprietor told us it wasn't funny at all, because someone did it every night. I think they fitted fixed seats that year, so it may have done some good in the end.

Our tutors arranged a football match between our college and a gaggle of undergrads from Oxford University. I was not picked, for which I was very glad, as I was scared of pain. I will describe the scene.

It had been raining for about three days. Mud was excessive. The match started off OK and our team was winning, when I think there was a bad tackle or some remark. It really did become a mud bath then. All joined in and the poor ref just gave up. The pitch was on a plateau with a steep slope running down to the lake. Fellows were rolling down into the lake. That didn't stop the fighting which started some pushing and shoving among the spectators. Well, I don't like pain, but with the name of our college at stake, we all joined in.

This was the best football match we ever had. It wasn't a punch-up. We were all laughing and quite good friends. The showers had never been used so much, and after a slap-up meal, we parted good friends.

In the dormitories on the third floor at the college, there was no fire escape, so harnesses had been provided and were hanging high up at every window. We were forbidden to touch them, which of course made us inquisitive as to how they worked.

There was dare and double-dare as to who was going to put one on and go down to try it out. It fell to Smithy to have a go, so eventually when we had worked out how to put it on, and I was all strapped up, they opened the window and I gingerly let myself down.

Halfway down, still moving, I started to swing like a pendulum. All was going pretty well, considering, until I suddenly noticed the principal walking along below, looking at a sheaf of papers. It was like the film The Great Escape. I froze, but was still swinging and all my mates were crowded at the windows looking down. There was so much laughing going on that the principal looked up and saw me. Pandemonium broke out. I had to continue my descent, as I did not know how to go back up and anyway I think these harnesses were only designed to go down.

When I reached the ground, all trussed up and unable to move, he let loose a torrent of words, and I realised I had done something wrong. I was grounded for a week.

Just after that the principal decided that we should know how the harnesses worked, and everyone had to take part in a fire drill. Can you imagine 500 students all running about, some coming down in harnesses from the top floor, being jerked about, some coming down the fire escape from the floor below, and others pouring out of the doors, not knowing which direction to go. It was chaos. It should have taken half an hour, but two hours later fellows were still running about trying to find where they were supposed to be. So my exploit did actually show how bad it would be if we really had a fire, and from then on we had regular fire drills, though somewhat better organised.

When I finished at Rycotewood, it was back to work with

a vengeance at Potters. The service of visiting farms doing specialised welding on big machines which could not really be moved, was unique in Oxfordshire at that time.

All summer I was kept busy, some weeks I never went back to the depot. I was going from farm to farm welding big jobs and small. I enjoyed it very very much.

6

Apprenticeship

The work eased off in late autumn, so back to the workshop I had to go, and work on the machinery. One morning, the foreman said, "Go to Brill and collect a Massey Harris combine, and drive it back to the works for an overhaul, Mike."

Well, it had been standing in this barn since the harvest before last. I checked the oil and water and kicked the tyres and then I was ready for the off. These combines had two design faults. One was the 14-foot cutter bar on the front. In those days the roads were not as wide as they are today, so meeting a car was a bit of a problem - but I always won! The second fault was that the machine was steered by the wheels at the rear, so when you turned the steering wheel, say, to the left, the back came out to the right and took up the whole road. Similarly, when you turned on the other lock, the rear wheels ended up on the pavement.

On this particular day, I arrived at the bottom end of Thame High Street. This street is the widest High Street in England, so wide that the car park was in the middle of the road and usually full, as it was this morning. The houses at the bottom of the High Street were quite close together, so I got a beautiful rasping exhaust note as I passed them. It was my duty, so I thought, to keep operating the accelerator, because on these combines, they had a straight through exhaust, meaning no silencer or muffler. The six cylinder engine did its duty well.

I got opposite the car park and spotted a group of girls standing by the Post Office waiting for the bus. I was doing my showing off, when the whole combine started to windmill. The machinery began to operate, and out of the back flew straw, chaff, dead mice and a terrific amount of dust. All the cars got nicely covered, together with the street, plus all the girls. I wished the road would open up and swallow me, but I had to carry on. The reason it started working was that the whole implement was driven by belts. They had been standing so long that they had stretched. When they got warm they contracted and dug into the pulleys and away it went.

I continued on to where I had to turn off the High Street, driving between a car showroom and a house. The gap, we know, was 15 foot and the cutter bar was 14 foot. Usually we had a lot of manoeuvring to do to get through, but today, with the adrenalin pumping, I got through in one (6 inches on each side) and even missed the telegraph pole strategically placed to catch any unwary driver. I waited days for the repercussions, but thankfully none came.

We used to have a tractor called an International Farm-All M. It had lovely brakes, which were made up of bands, and when they were operated, the gorgeous noise of brakes screeching turned everyone's head, especially girls'. They could not understand why the brake bands wore out in six months. I knew!

Another day in my life, I was sent out to a combine because it wouldn't move when a gear was selected, so big-head knew.

"Gear box," I thought. "Right, take the gear box out and take it back to the workshop where all the special tools are."

In removing the box, the belts and adjusters had to be removed, so back in the workshop I stripped it down and found the broken part. The stores had to order a part and it would not be there until the next afternoon. When it came, I quickly rebuilt the box and loaded it into my pick-up truck and returned to the combine, feeling very puffed up with myself, because I'd used my common sense and got the job done in very good time at just 17 years old.

Imagine the scene if you can. The machine had been working the day before and the farmer had left a beautiful square of uncut wheat. The field was on a slope and the machine had broken down on the top side of the field, facing across the field, so it was time for a "road test" as I called it. Starting the engine, I selected the first gear. As it moved, I changed gears and tried reverse. Everything was working perfectly. I thought, "I'll do a complete cut of this square," so I started off going down the field. We were going faster than I thought we should have been. I applied the brakes, which were always awful on a Massey Harris, this one being no exception. Instead of stopping, we seemed to go faster. Panic set in. I thought, "What can I do? If I continue straight down I will hit those elm trees, so I had better turn across the field through the uncut wheat and head uphill to slow myself down." So that is what I did.

By this time I realised what I had not done, namely, I had not adjusted the tension on the belts. I did this quickly and drove the combine to the top of the field and left it in the same spot. I picked up my tools, and loaded them in the van and raced down onto the main road, which ran parallel to the field, allowing you to look up at it. There was the beautiful square, still there, with a very artistic curve running through the middle of it. Of course I had to own up to it, which caused great joviality in the workshop amongst the mechanics. I never lived that one down.

Back at work, I had the chance of overhauling my first engine. I was so thrilled at this and soon got to work removing parts, washing and cleaning them, and stacking them in boxes.

Finally, when all that was done, it was time to scrape off the old gaskets. This job takes ages, so, being a lazy lad, I looked around for an easy way of doing it. Out came the welding torch. Things were going well, I thought, the gaskets were falling off with the heat.

Half way through the job, the foreman saw what I was doing. He went mad. I was astonished as I was sure he would be pleased that I was ahead of time, but no. I had a lecture on expansion and contraction in small places. You see, heat concentrated in one place expands just in that one place, and when it cools down, it buckles. He proved it too, by laying a straight edge over the cooled parts and showed that oil would be gushing out, no matter how many new gaskets one fitted. The firm had to buy new parts, but they still let me build up the engine and it worked perfectly. Still, I cost the firm a lot of money.

It was rotten of us I know, and I feel rather ashamed of it now, but it was a laugh at the time - every new lad that came to work there had the same treatment as follows...

We sent them to the stores department for stupid things, such as a glass-head hammer, glass nails, a box of sparks, a set of sky hooks, and one of the best ones was a tin of 'Clinkit'. While the lad was on his way to the stores, we phoned the storeman to expect him, so all was pre-arranged. The storeman obtained an empty tin, filled it a quarter full with water and a handful of old nuts and bolts. The lid was replaced, and the lad would walk into the stores and ask the storeman for a "tin of Clinkit." The storeman would say, "Do they want to use it now?"

"I guess so," said the lad.

"Well you must shake the tin all the time until you reach the workshop," said the storeman.

We all heard him leave the stores, all the way to the workshop, and the blokes would say, "How long has this been shaken?"

"Since I left the stores," said the boy.

One bloke looked at the clock and said thoughtfully, "It's not quite long enough. Stand there and shake the tin until I say 'stop'."

Poor kid, when we took the lid off, there were hoots of laughter, and the lad had a very red face. I didn't see why they laughed so much as they had seen it done several times before. I know I was caught when I first went there. They also sent me for the long weight. I thought it was a heavy piece of metal, but of course it really was a long WAIT.

My firm sent me out on a tractor to a farm, to collect a manure spreader. The tractor itself had trouble with the governors, which governed the engine and kept the speed down. If you opened the throttle, the engine would rev at full bore, and the tractor would shoot forward at high speed. It would reach almost 35 mph, an unheard of speed for a tractor, and also illegal, but speed to me in those days was wonderful. The tractor was an International Farm-All M. It was designed for having implements attached for hoeing the ground etc. It was also used for road work, because its normal speed was higher than most field tractors.

I arrived at the farm, found the manure spreader, and hooked it up to the tractor. There was a shaft that made the tractor drive the manure spreader mechanism. It was connected but not operating. The manure spreader had two spinners with paddles fitted to them. This picked up the manure from the container and threw it out from the back to a fair distance across the field. It was out of operation when I was towing it, but could be slipped into gear by manipulating your foot and pressing down on a lever.

I proceeded along the road at a high rate of knots, glanced behind me and saw a black, highly polished police car following me and ringing his bell for me to stop. I pretended not to hear. I wasn't going to lose my newly acquired driving licence, so I pressed the gear lever with my foot, and the machine came alive. All the sloppy manure was flung far and wide, and ended up all over the police car and the road.

There were no windscreen washers on cars in those days. When they turned the wipers on, they made it worse. The blobs of manure became a widespread mess, and they could not see past it. I made a fast getaway. I knew the geography of the area, and remembered that just round the corner was a field adjacent to the road with a tall thick hedge running alongside the road. So while the police were trying to clean their windows, I shot into the field, and waited behind the hedge. After about 10 minutes, I heard the police car go past, ringing their bell, so I thought, "Right, this is a farm tractor. I could go cross-country to the works over the fields."

Well, I did not know how many fields there were exactly. Some of them had gates in them that had never been opened for years, so that took ages, opening and closing. Eventually, I came out onto an old lane, so I journeyed back to the works with an empty manure spreader (I did them a favour there) and a tractor covered in mud.

The foreman was jumping up and down wondering where I was, because where the incident happened was only 10 minutes from the works, but it took me over two and a half hours cross-country, as the crow wobbles! He made me wash both the tractor and the spreader until they were spotlessly clean. I always thought my firm valued me highly, but now I look back I am not so sure.

Also, I realised it was one thing to torment Mr Plod, but quite a different thing to come up against the real police force.

I can remember one day which I shall never forget. This is more serious now. It had snowed quite hard during the day while I was at work. After work we had a snowball fight and a good time was had by all. I mounted my old motorbike and set off for home in the snow.

In those days we didn't have crash hats or goggles and the snow was stinging my eyes. The roads became an ice rink. You see, there were no salt gritters. All the councils did was to spread gravel on the roads here and there, so of course the snow did not melt at all, and it became compacted and very slippery. Snow and ice built up on the head lamps. In those days lighting was awful at the best of times, and the light emitted was no better than a glow worm.

Well, I was riding along the A40 with my head down trying to shield my eyes a little. My feet were dragging along the road, keeping the bike upright. At one point I lifted my head and to my horror, not 15 yards away, I came upon a lorry broken down, so my first reaction was to brake, and of course the bike and I parted company. The motorbike ended up under the lorry and I carried on overtaking it on my backside, gently pirouetting on my way past. I began spinning like a top. The driver got out of his cab and helped me up just as I parked myself against the kerb on the other side of the road. I was so lucky that night. There was no traffic, but roads were quiet then.

We pulled my bike out from under the lorry. It didn't look too bad. What a fool I was in those days, for I helped to get the lorry's engine started. All the driver said was "Thanks mate" and he drove off. I was left to push the bike home uphill, slipping and sliding. I thought then, "He didn't even give me half a crown for my trouble." Still, you live and learn.

My brother wasn't as lucky as me. He also rode a motorbike. His was faster and bigger than mine. He worked at a big Ford garage in Aylesbury and had started courting Daphne.

That morning it was freezing and very thick fog, and he was late for work, so of course he tried to go a little faster than was safe in those conditions. Well, out of the fog loomed this car standing in the middle of the road, with the driver scraping his windscreen. John's first reaction was to brake, and of course the bike went from under him, and catapulted him into the path of a car coming in the opposite direction. I can't remember what the bike hit, but it was in a mess.

At any rate, I got a phone call from the office, telling me about the accident. My parents must have phoned in. The boss of the firm was a very strict and aloof person, but this day he said, "Take one of the lorries and visit your brother in hospital, and bring his bike back to the works."

There was only one lorry in the pound and it was brand new, so the foreman said I could use that. I'd never driven a lorry before. It was an Austin 3-tonner flat bed, so I set off to Aylesbury. I reached the crash scene. The police were still there. They were very co-operative, and helped me to load the bike onto the lorry. They showed me the car that my brother hit with his body. It was owned by one of his firm's customers, and we found out later it was brand new and the repairs cost £300, which was a lot of money in those days. The police escorted me to the hospital by driving in front, and they made sure there was room in the car park to accommodate the lorry.

Mum and Dad were there at John's bedside. They told me the extent of his injuries, the main one of which was a shattered left arm. The doctors were undecided whether to amputate his arm, but fortune was on his side that day, for a lady surgeon was visiting the hospital and was interested in his arm. She said she could rebuild it, and good as her word, she did rebuild it, and to this day he has silver plates in his arm, which is rather a funny shape. We were all very grateful to the surgeon. Now, if we need a bank loan, we can use John as collateral, because of the silver plates!

When he came out of hospital, John had his arm in a plaster cast, bent across his chest. Instantly he set about repairing his motorbike. He was told before he left the hospital not to use his left hand or try to move his arm, but he ignored that. After a couple of days, his plaster became very dirty with oily patches, and it was cracked at the elbow and very ragged at the wrist. Mother had to wrap it in old sheets when he went to bed, to keep the bedclothes clean. Today we might have put it in a plastic bag, but they had not been invented then. Every time he went to the hospital for a check up they used to tell him off severely and change the plaster, but it made no difference to him. He was mad.

He had to go into Rycotewood College to take some City and Guilds exams while he was in plaster. He did all the workings out jotted down on his plaster, and what with dabs of oil in between, it looked like a map of the world, because he used different coloured pens. He was very courageous and hard working, and a first class mechanic, but obstinate.

He finished his motorcycle and rode it again with his plaster on. He used to pull his whole body forward to get at the clutch lever with his left hand, because he couldn't straighten his arm out. After the motorbike, he tackled the farm tractor, which needed a new clutch. I could not help as I had to go to work. He dismantled the tractor, and changed the clutch with one good hand and arm - a fantastic achievement.

Looking around for another job, his eye fell upon a Wolseley 14. Father had taken it in part payment for some wheat. The chassis was like a rusty colander - Father was cheated there. My brother set to work. He removed the complete body of the car, then the engine and gearbox. He borrowed some welding equipment from I don't know where. He cut out the rusted metal, made up new pieces and let them in, and welded them together. He made a superb job of it. He did it by himself except for lifting awkward heavy bits, where we all lent a hand. It did not sag in the middle anymore when he had finished. It was a lovely old car, and before he repaired it, somehow I had taken my driving test in it! This is how it came about...

An hour before the test, my brother, who had already passed his test, took me round the circuit they used. He was showing me the manoeuvres. The last one was an emergency stop.

He said, "When I slap the dashboard, you slam on the brakes."

He hit the dashboard, and I hit the brakes. Fine for a second or two, and then the brake pedal reached the floor boards! We had split one of the hydraulic brake pipes. The brakes were useless.

My brother sent me round to the test centre to explain I would be a bit late, due to the brakes packing up, and he crawled underneath, located the broken brake pipe, twisted it round and round and squeezed it together with some mole-grips (rather like pliers). They were left on all the time while I took my test. My brother turned up at the test centre with the car and my examiner was very impressed that it was working - we didn't tell him it only had three brakes, as he might have refused to come out in it.

Off we went, doing the circuit, and it started to snow heavily. He pulled me into a lay-by to ask me some questions on the Highway Code - as they did then. I was very nervous, what with one thing and another. He asked me the sequence of the traffic lights, and after I spent five minutes on it, he said, "I don't know what part of the country you come from, but here we stop at red, we wait a little for amber, and we go on green, but having heard your explanation I am thoroughly confused. However, we will let it go and continue with the test, but are you sure these brakes are all right?"

So I demonstrated by pumping my foot up and down while stationary, giving him a false sense of security. He then went on to give me an emergency stop, and to my amazement, it worked OK.

In those days, we had to drive with the window down, to show we knew the hand signals, as only a few cars had electric indicators, and what they had was only a yellow arrow, which shot up on the driver's side. You still had to do hand signals to turn left. The Wolseley had no indicators, so the window was permanently open. After I had done the hand signals, he said, "I don't know if you were a drowning whale, or if you were waving to your mum."

We got back on the physical driving test again with the snow still falling. We were going along quite nicely (in my opinion) when a lady on a bike in front of us suddenly skidded on the snow, and fell off into the road.

I could see out of the corner of my eye, the examiner stiffen and stamp on the floor as if he had a brake there, wondering what I would do. I had already decided I had failed the test with the traffic light question, so I was fairly relaxed, having given up. I pulled out gently around the lady lying in the road, apparently asleep. I didn't use the brakes at all, having little faith in them. I didn't panic, doing a wide arc round the lady, and pulled up at the kerb, doing my drowning man act with the hand signals. I got out of the car and went back and helped her and the bike onto the pavement. She assured me she was OK and with a careless attitude, convinced I had not passed, I sauntered back to the car.

The examiner was still sitting there. I don't think he was dead, but he handed me my pass certificate. I could not speak, but I managed to say eventually, "I'll drive you back to the test centre."

He said, "Don't bother. I'll walk from here. It's bad enough being on snow, without having only three brakes. Wait there. I will send your brother to you."

When we got back home we had a ceremony burning the L plates as we could all drive now, except Mum, who refused to learn - in fact not many women drove then, probably because there was usually only one car in the family. In fact, not many families had a car. Mum could drive the tractor, and that was more important.

When I finished my apprenticeship and got my qualifications, my parents bought me a watch. I was very proud of it, because watches were quite expensive then, and not everyone had one. I used to roll my left sleeve up a bit and wave my arm around so people would see I had a watch. But oh, tragedy was to come!

Some makes of combines were delivered to Potters partly assembled, via the railway. I had about six of these combines to finish off. One of the jobs was to fit a canvas conveyor from the cutter bar up into the threshing drum. Everything was going fine, and I realised I might scratch my watch if I carried on. I took it off my wrist and laid it on the conveyor, and carried on fitting and adjusting.

Eventually I finished and now the combine had its own engine, independent of a tractor, so I started it up in order to test the speeds etc and to make sure it would be able to go out to a farmer and be used straight away. This also was run on drive belts. The engine was running beautifully, so I started to engage the clutch, and everything started to move as it should do, getting faster and faster.

Suddenly, I looked at the canvas, just in time to see my beautiful wrist watch disappear into the threshing drum. Then there was that horrible BANG! Out of the back came little bits of broken glass, metal, cogs and springs. That brought me down to size, didn't it?

During the winter months on the farm we had to feed supplements to the cows, such as hay, straw, and cow cabbage, that is kale. It was the job for us boys to distribute the food to the cows. That involved loading the cart with kale first, and then wurzel mangels - they are like big swedes.

John was driving the tractor, with me on top of the load. Everything was just fine for a while, until we hit a very large bump. I was throwing the mangels out one at a time - they were about the size of a football. Well, this bump shot me in the air just as I launched a mangel into the air. It sailed up quite high and then came down and impaled itself on the horns of one of the cows. The cow was a bit surprised, but carried on eating as if nothing had happened, until all the mangels were eaten.

The rest of the cows must have seen or smelt the one that was left on her horn and they followed her all over the field trying to get it off, or at least get a bite. I think the poor old cow must have been worn out, so we took pity on her and hooked it off with a long stick and she devoured it herself without letting the others get a look in.

Winter gave way to spring and it was lambing time. We had to round up all the pregnant ewes and try to coax them into an empty open barn. We used to think what stupid animals they were, because we would get them to the entrance, and then one would jump an imaginary fence, and that would spook the rest, so they scattered and round-up began again. We won at last and then it was to work, lambing in the cold night air by lanterns, as you remember we had no electricity.

Once the lambs were born, the mothers' feelings changed and they became very protective of their offspring and very good mothers. In the morning, after they were dry, all the newborns began playing among themselves. When they got older, they became more and more frisky and pretty. It was a shame they had to grow up into stupid sheep.

My father, for once in his life, lashed out and bought a modern car. It was a Wolseley 6/80. OK, I'll come clean. It was a second-hand ex-police car, like the one I sprayed with you-know-what. It was a lovely looking car and when the lights were turned on, a small light came on in the middle of the radiator grille, showing the 'Wolseley' name. The police were still using them as their patrol cars, in fact they were still current.

One evening, at dusk, John and I had to drive into Oxford. We were still running on sidelights and everyone thought it was a police car because of the grille light. In those days lorries were limited to 20 mph so we had a bit of fun in driving up to the rear of a lorry, and as soon as the driver saw us in his mirror, we saw his speed drop from 40 to 20 mph quite quickly. Then we overtook and the poor old driver had to build up speed again, which took him quite a while. It was naughty but good fun.

Now come the worst days of my life. They were when we had to leave the farm for good. You see, my parents realised both John and I didn't like farming, working seven days a week, nearly 24 hours a day, especially in the winter in the cold and mud. We loved cars and engines, so we moved from Oxfordshire to Gloucestershire.

My parents bought a garage on Cleeve Hill, Cheltenham, and we started working seven days a week, nearly 24 hours a day in a different work! (stupid or what?) So that ended our farming life and this account of our life there.

Part II

Memoirs of a Cotswold Mechanic
(Or More Don't Try This at Home!)

7

Moving On

A sad day dawned in the mid 1950s for my brother and me. We left the farm at Tetsworth, which had been our home during our childhood. Now that both of us were apprenticed to the motor trade, our parents had decided it was time to move from the farm which had given us many happy times, but also a great deal of hard graft, working long hours in the cold and mud.

They had bought a small garage on Cleeve Hill, just outside Cheltenham in Gloucestershire. It sold petrol and had a large but shabby workshop down the slope below. The views were glorious across the valley to the Malvern Hills in the distance. However, we had not come to gaze at the views. The task of building up the trade would take 24 hours a day, 7 days a week. How would this be better than the farm? Time would tell.

We couldn't afford a removal van to move all our belongings, so we had to move it by car and trailer. This took several trips. We had to work in the garage during the day, and then at night go back to the farm to load up the trailer and then back to Cleeve Hill. One night John was on his way back when the trailer draw bar broke. The trailer was of course grossly overloaded. It was dark, so all he could do was to drag it up onto the grass alongside the road and leave it there. We were all worried, but when we went back to it, we found that no one had tampered with it. We set to and repaired the draw bar. Imagine if it was the present day. The trailer would probably have gone, along with most of our goods.

The only accommodation on Cleeve Hill was a small, cold caravan, which we boys shared, and a living area, which we partitioned off in the office building for Mum and Dad. Every morning we had to fold everything up and put it in a big cupboard in there. There was no chance of a lie-in. We were always up by 6 am and did not get to bed until almost midnight. The door of the office building was falling off and had to be repaired, along with many other jobs. The floor of the workshop was compacted earth, so we concreted it by hand in sections, as and when we could afford it.

There were no car hoists, so we had to do everything on trolley jacks - very dangerous. We were prompted to get a hoist by an accident that happened one day. I was lying underneath a jacked-up car, trying to remove an exhaust, which was well and truly rusted on. I was pulling and pushing as hard as I could. I thought the car was safe, and wouldn't move, but it did, and fell down onto its wheels, trapping me beneath, but with the protruding bolt penetrating my ear, fortunately only by about a quarter of an inch. (I still have the scar and charge 50p + VAT to see it.) My father and brother heard me shout, and rushed to lift the car off me bodily. This accident was my own fault. I should have used axle stands or blocks, so if the car fell, they would have supported it, but we could not afford axle stands. We were penniless.

During the war, my father had worked on Rolls Royce Merlin aircraft engines, but unfortunately, despite his experience, not many dropped in for a service, so he became our gofer (go for this and go for that). He also did taxi work, which was a legacy from the previous owner.

Of course, at this time we were still apprentices, our apprenticeships having been transferred to Victory Motors in Cheltenham. We worked there during the day, and at our own garage evenings and weekends. Mum kept the books, and served petrol.

Two old ladies regarded the taxi service as their personal chauffeur. Both of them would ring up for Dad and keep him waiting while they did their shopping. He would return hours later, with about five shillings. Both of them were very rich and had property all over the town, but they were very mean, and did not even give him a drink. One of them especially, a Miss Hastings, had a lot of houses in the town, and could have afforded her own car, but she wanted someone to open the door and touch their cap to her. It made us very angry and eventually we gave up the taxi service.

When we bought the workshop, included in the deal was a 1937 Talbot. We joked about the long bonnet, saying it was 40,000 miles long. It was the car used for the taxi. One of the old ladies had hired it to go to the South of France the year before we got there. We also inherited the previous owner's chauffeur. He would drive it all over Europe. I personally wouldn't have driven it down Cleeve Hill. It had cable brakes, which meant it veered either one side or the other, so it had to be fixed nearly every day. I was thinking of putting a FORD badge on it - Fixed Often, Repaired Daily, but my brother, having been apprenticed to a Ford dealer, was not so keen.

It was a blighter to start at any time. The chauffeur seemed to be able to start it OK, but we had no end of trouble. Unfortunately he had a heart attack and died, so we had to tackle the car ourselves.

There was no heater, and one cold day, Mum took a booking from Miss Hastings to take her into town straight away. Dad should have been back much earlier, but he did not appear, so I had to drive her. What a waste of time! I duly arrived at her house and she came out in her fur coat and pearls, etc. She was rather a stout lady and when she sat in the car, she said haughtily, "Put the blanket round me." No please or thank you. So, not knowing exactly what to do, I considered carefully. The car was very big, large enough nearly to hold a dance in the back, so I put one foot on the running board, and was stretching across with the blanket, when I lost my balance, and landed up head first into the deep cushions on the back seat. She was very put out, and said, "Stop fooling about and stand up and get out and do the driving at once." When I looked in the mirror, she looked like a big fat pig, wrapped up in the blanket.

It must have been one of those days, because everything went wrong. I dropped her off in the High Street (it was not pedestrianised then and was two-way traffic). She did her shopping and out she came eventually, followed by two or three assistants carrying her purchases. That meant I had to get out of the car in the cold and open the boot, with her instructing me in her commanding manner how to load them in there. Then we had to follow the rigmarole of getting her in and tucking the blanket round her. From that moment on I decided to refuse to take her ever again.

To continue, I started to drive off and wanted to turn up Winchcombe Street. I changed from first gear to second, to third, then started to slow down. I changed into second gear, and all of a sudden the car stopped absolutely dead in its tracks. The fat old lady came hurtling forward onto the back rest of the front seat. I realised what had happened. Something had gone wrong in the gearbox, so we got two gears at once. She gave me a torrent of abuse: "Why did you brake so hard?" I explained about the gears, but she wouldn't or couldn't listen, and that was the last straw.

A deep hatred developed between us. I said, "You had better catch the bus home."

So she said, "You had better run me round to the bus station."

"Madam," I said, "I cannot move the car."

By this time, Mr Plod appeared on the scene.

"You can't stop here," he said.

I said, "I wouldn't park here, even if you paid me, but the gearbox has gone wrong."

So he said, "You had better move it and quick."

So you can imagine I was pretty bad tempered, having idiots talk to me.

I threw the keys at Mr Plod and said, "If you can do better than me, feel free."

Then the old woman started up again. She said to Mr Plod, "He stopped dead and refused to move on."

So Mr Plod had a bit of sympathy for her, but none for me, and the old Talbot didn't let me down - she refused to start. He continued pressing the starter button, so eventually the battery became flat, and said, "It won't go."

I said, "No, you've flattened the battery for me. Thank you very much."

He got out and said, "I can't stay here. I've got to go."

The old woman was whining in the background, so I said, "Well, take her with you."

She raised the issue of her parcels, so the policeman said he would get a taxi for her. She informed me in no uncertain terms that she never wanted to travel with me again.

That was just fine by me. We later rang up Shakespeare's

Taxis in Winchcombe and very kindly passed her on to him. Strangely, he never thanked us for this trade!

I went into Steels Garage nearby and asked to use their phone. My brother said he would bring some tools down, and we set to in the middle of the High Street removing the carpets and trims and removing the top of the gearbox to ascertain what had gone wrong. We soon found the trouble. It was a collar which had split in half and fallen down into the gearbox. Fortunately, my brother had brought a reel of wire, so we wired the half collar back where it should be and used yards of wire holding it together temporarily.

The old lady was still enthroned in the back, listening to mechanics' vocabulary and moaning that the taxi had not come to pick her up. Eventually it came, and she was bundled into the back of his car and they set off to Cleeve Hill, only to realise, when they were almost there, that she had left the parcels in our boot.

They started coming back down Cleeve Hill. Meantime, we had finished the repair and set off back up the hill. Unfortunately, we did not notice them as we passed them, because John was in the Wolseley, and I was driving cautiously, hoping the wire would hold, so when they arrived in the High Street, we had gone, and they had to drive back up to Cleeve Hill again! That was the end of my taxiing, mutually agreed by all involved.

We managed to sell the Talbot. A school teacher with a big family fell in love with it, and took it away. My brother thought, "How thick can anyone be?" But there, one man's meat is another man's poison.

Cleeve Hill was new to me, and I didn't know anyone and was very shy, so as for friends, I had none, but that didn't stop me seeing the funny side of things, such as a lady customer coming into the garage complaining about her car running rough and using a lot of petrol.

We went through all the checks but we couldn't find a thing wrong with it. She came to collect her car and we were talking about this, when she told us she had already visited five other garages, and they couldn't find anything wrong either, so off she went.

Next day she was on the phone giving us a bad time, so we said, "Bring the car back and we will give you a lift back to your house in Winchcombe."

She duly arrived. We all talked about the problem and in the end I got into the passenger seat and she got into the driver's seat. That was when I saw what the problem was. I sat there laughing like mad. She turned to me and asked why I was laughing.

"Have I dressed wrongly?" she said.

"No," I said, "but I can see what you are doing wrong that's causing all your engine problems."

"Oh, what's that?" she said.

"Well," I said, "when you got into the driver's seat, the first thing you did was to pull the choke knob out and hang your handbag on it."

I took the handbag off and pushed the choke in and the engine ran sweetly. We all had a good laugh about it.

She said, "When I bought the car, I thought how clever the makers were to think of the ladies' needs." She then became the longest serving customer we had.

8

National Service

One day, over the airways, came the news that Nasser, the president of Egypt, had blockaded the Suez Canal, scuttling ships in order to prevent sea traffic getting through. This meant an oil shortage worldwide. Petrol was put on ration, which hit garages, as people could hardly use their cars at all.

Victory Motors decided to get rid of their apprentices. John had already finished and was working full time at Cleeve Hill, but my apprenticeship was ended abruptly. Now I look back, I am sure that was illegal, but at the time I was glad to be able to work full time at home in the garage.

No sooner had I started than a bombshell dropped through the post in a brown envelope with OHMS on it. I opened it up and found I had to report to Gloucester, which I didn't know at all. It was my call-up papers, to do National Service in the Army for two years. All lads of 18 years old had to do it, but if you were doing an apprenticeship it was deferred until you had finished. I was devastated.

John did not have to go because his left arm had been rebuilt with silver plates and was twisted and a little weak, so the medical department rejected him. I unfortunately passed the medical.

Then came the regiment selection. They said we had a choice, but when it came to it, they dictated where we were going. I asked to go in the REME, which was the engineering section, but they said, "Definitely not. It is full up."

The way I was feeling, I could have hit the little whipper-snapper. He said they would let me know what regiment I would be in. I stormed out and made my way home to Cheltenham. Sure enough, a letter came, which said "your new regiment will be the Household Cavalry." My heart sank and I thought, "Oh no, not horses."

They gave me a train ticket to get to Windsor. When I duly arrived, hacked off and nervous, I shall never forget walking through the iron gates of Combermere Barracks, Windsor. There, in front of me, a big corporal of horse, equal to a ser-geant, was bellowing at me. I didn't understand what he was saying. I thought to myself at the time, "I'll keep my eye on you, you non-entity." Only one thing wrong - he was going to be my drill instructor, so that didn't go down very well.

We had to go for another medical within the perimeter of our camp in the middle of Windsor. Imagine the scene - plate glass alongside the pavement, waiting to have our injections, and they were using the same needle all the way along the line. We didn't think much of that, as it got blunter and blunter as they went along. That would not be allowed today on the grounds of infection.

That over, we were marched to the stores to get our new kit, ie clothes, hat, boots, etc. We had three hats - one a beret, which was two sizes too small, a khaki cap about three sizes too big, and a red and blue forage cap, about five sizes too big. Then there were two sets of hobnail boots, supposed to be my size, but larger, and two battle suits. Then we were marched to the tailor and his large number of staff. They descended on us with chalk and tape measures and proceeded to alter the badly fitting garments. The question came into everyone's minds: "Why didn't they give us the right size in the first place?"

Next day we got a call to collect our clothes and this was called 'the first fitting'. You have never seen such a mess in your life. There were seams splitting open, blokes with big stomachs hanging over their trousers, some of us with sleeves covering our hands as we stood to attention, and boots that pinched and hurt. And now comes the funny bit with boots. We couldn't see any point in this whatsoever, except to demoralise us. We had to get a lit candle, heat up our eating spoon on the handle end, and burn off the little pimples on the boots until they were dead smooth. Then came the hard work - small-circling with boot polish. This took forever, working on them late into the night, even after 'lights-out'. After the kit was cleaned and polished, everything had to be kept pressed, polished, blancoed, etc. What a waste of time. This was the worst time of my life, wasting time when I should have been back at the garage building up the business. However, I made up my mind to try and see the funny side of things as much as I could.

The food in the Army was nothing like home cooking. Even the vegetables were hard like stones. They had huge urns of tea, which tasted like fermented beer, and when we went out for a route march, they cut us sandwiches. Each slice was about two inches thick. The filling - well we never did know what it was. It all sent me reminiscing about my school days, when we had beautiful food cooked by Mrs Summersby and her staff. She cooked for four schools and all the pupils came to her to eat in a rota, in the big hall. She ruled her staff nicely but firmly - nothing we had was unpalatable. Her treacle puddings and spotted dicks were out of this world. We used to go back for seconds if we could. She was a lovely old lady and she had four children of her own of various ages, and she spoke to us the same as to her family, with "duckys" and "dears" sprinkled everywhere. What a shock it was to have Army food. The officers and NCOs had their own mess, or food hall, and their food was much better than ours.

We spent hours marching backwards and forwards, jumping up and down, saluting, rifle drill - all to my way of thinking, being used like tin soldiers by the NCOs. They were trying to break our morale and turn us into robots, but they didn't succeed. Like many of the others, I made up my mind to do as little as possible, be decent to my fellow inmates and be very, very wary of all NCOs and officers. When volunteers were called for, one trick us old sweats did on parade was to take one step backwards, leaving the new intake at the mercy of the NCOs. We learned that because it had been done to us.

They taught us map-reading and grid references in the classroom. Then they took us out on exercises in a truck with the tonneau cover tightly tied down, so we did not know where we were going, but we were driving for about an hour. That was a bit of a worry. They gave us a grid reference and a map and put us in groups and we had to find our way to where the truck had gone on to. They dumped us out and to my surprise we were on the Chiltern Hills, near Chinnor. I knew this area well, because it was near Tetsworth, our childhood home. All the other guys had no idea where they were, so my group had a huge advantage. They were not entirely convinced of this, as I often got things wrong, but I knew exactly where we were.

It was a lovely hot day and the rest of my group was trying to work out their whereabouts with pencils and rulers, but I set off straight away, without looking at the map. I knew exactly where we were going to be picked up - at Nettlebed, at the foot of the Chilterns, near Dorchester. I was able to take things nice and easy, even stopping at a village shop and buying a bottle of Tizer, which I had to get rid of before I reached the truck. I reached the truck in record time.

The NCOs and the officer were so surprised, because I had always made out to be a thicky, in order to get out of doing anything. I was first back, and had the prize, which turned out to be a doorstep sandwich with cheese and meat in it. It was partially stale, because of the heat. They said, "Well, you're very good at map-reading, Smith," and I said, "Well, you've either got it or you haven't."

Little did they know that if they had taken me somewhere else, I would have been last back. The next time we had to do map-reading, they told me I was driving the vehicle, as I was the only one with a full licence, so this was easy-peasy for me. I had an officer map-reading in the passenger seat. He got it wrong several times, and as it was also in my area, near Aylesbury, I was able to put him right. He also thought I was a marvellous map-reader. I didn't let on!

Part of our training was learning battle craft on Bagshot Heath. We spent a week learning how to ambush people and to camouflage ourselves and our equipment, etc. The last night, a small group sat round a log fire. The NCOs and officers were in large tents, asleep. We had some thunder flashes which were to take the place of hand grenades - they were giant fireworks really, and went off with a very loud bang. There were about 15 NCOs and officers, all asleep, and we had a plan of campaign, and that was to creep up on their tents at a set time, wait two minutes until everyone was in place, and then lift the flap of the tent, set the thunder flashes to explode in 30 seconds, and throw them into the tents. Then we made a quick getaway into a thicket of wood and gorse. Two of us only just made it in time.

There was a series of loud explosions and men shouting. Then they came running out of the tents with clouds of smoke following them. We had no sleep for the rest of that night. Next morning we recruits were rounded up and put on a charge, because none of us would own up to doing this wonderful deed. We were all due to go on embarkation leave that day. We cleaned our kit and handed it back into the stores. Then we went up before the CO (commanding officer) to answer the charge. The NCOs and officers were standing to attention and we were brought to attention in front of the colonel. We thought he would hand down a stiff sentence to all of us, so we expected the worst.

He asked who brought the charge. The two officers took one step forward, meaning them, at which the colonel proceeded to give them a right good dressing down. He asked us if we had anything to say. I couldn't help myself for saying, "We only paid them back for doing it to us all the past week."

Then he said, "You have taught these young officers a very good lesson, and that is to post a guard when they are sleeping. Case dismissed."

It was just about midday by now and we were all tired and wanted to get home on leave. I got my motorbike out and rode it through Windsor, Slough, and up to Beaconsfield to meet up with the main A40 road. I found that if you travelled at 30 or 60 mph through Slough, you could hit every traffic light on green. I can remember turning left towards Oxford and the next thing I remembered was a huge jolt. I'd fallen asleep on the bike and woke up riding along the grass bank and over a trench, which woke me up. I can remember the look on a lorry driver's face as he passed me, coming in the opposite direction. I rode on until I kept dozing off again, when I saw a gateway in a field that had just been harvested, so I took a nap behind the hedge. The farmer woke me up and asked why I was there, so I told him and he took pity on me and gave me a drink of rough cider. I don't think this helped matters, because I can't remember the rest of the journey. However, I arrived home safely.

We finished our training and got away on embarkation leave. I think we had about 10 days, which flew by. My tummy was going over and over all the time, because we were to be sent to Cyprus.

There was a lot of trouble in Cyprus then, because the Greeks and the Turks who lived there both thought the island should belong to them, stirred up by a Greek Orthodox priest called Makarios. A terrorist organization called EOKA was setting bombs and shooting from balconies etc at British soldiers, who were there supposedly to keep the peace.

I travelled back to Windsor by steam train. We collected our kit and boarded lorries to be taken to an airport and loaded aboard. This was the first time I had ever flown. In a military aircraft they turned the seats around so we had our backs to the engine. A lot of us didn't like that and it made us quite ill. I got a seat looking out over a wing and engine. Being a trained mechanic, I became concerned when I saw engine oil streaming down the wing. I decided to tell one of the RAF NCSOs, but when I did I was told to sit down and not to spook everyone else, or I'd be put on a charge. I thought, "That doesn't matter, because if we crash into the sea it won't come to court in any case." Many years later when I got my flying licence, I found out from my instructor, who was an ex-RAF pilot with thousands of hours under his belt, that if the engine stopped spewing out oil, something was very wrong. I will tell you later about my time as a private pilot and my old instructor, John Cole.

We landed in Germany to refuel and top up the engine oil, took off again with the same oil leak and landed in Malta, where I had a bad dose of flu. I didn't tell anyone because if I had, they would have put me in hospital for a while, and after that I would have had to travel to Cyprus by boat. As you know, I was fond of water in ponds, but not now with a three-day trip, feeling seasick. So we flew on. When we had landed in Nicosia, they opened all the doors, and a blast of red-hot air shot into the cabin, along with all the flies in the world. I've never seen so many, or so large. This journey had taken 12 hours. We were shattered, but it did arouse my interest in flying.

We were taken by lorry to our camp. People were stripping off as we travelled, it was so hot, and we were wearing winter clothing. We reached camp, only to be bellowed at to get dressed, and of course the obligatory "you will be on a charge." I think those six words were the only words they have ever learned to speak consecutively. As you can see, I was very rebellious at that time. After all, I was taken away from my home and business to go out there and offer myself up to playing at soldiers. Things did get a little better when I was assigned to the Motor Transport section, so I made the best of a bad job.

The first vehicle I was given was a very old Bedford QL. It was used in the last war and it was OK, but I wanted a new Bedford RL, which was modern looking. What they didn't know at that time was that I was a mechanic and knew some of the tricks of the trade. How could I exchange my lorry? The first thing I did was to get a large bowl and a funnel and stow them on board. The detail that day was to go to Famagusta. About 10 miles out was a bit of a swamp with tall bamboo, which hid the lorry from the road so, as quick as I could, out came the bowl and funnel and the tool kit. Micky Mouse owned that, but I made quite sure I had a spanner to fit the sump plug. Having drained all the oil and put it into a sealed can, I proceeded on my way. The oil warning light shone big and bright. The old lorry sounded just the same as it always did and I continued out a few more miles. Then panic set in as I remembered a steep hill in my favour, so I put my foot down and got to the magic speed of 60 mph - all she would do. Halfway down the hill, I thought, "Here goes," as 60 mph was on the clock, then first gear was rammed in. It wasn't the engine that gave up - it was the gearbox. I coasted to the side of the road and refilled the engine with the oil without spilling a drop. A Land Rover stopped, and the NCO asked if I was OK. I said, "Not really. I have lost all the drive to the wheels, so could you get in touch with my camp?"

In time, a great big Scammel tow truck pulled up and lifted my old truck up and we were taken back to camp. A sergeant from the REME quizzed me on how it happened. I said, innocently, "I was going on very nicely when we came to a dead stop. Do you think it could be the engine that has gone wrong?"

The sergeant said he had to check the oil in the engine as a matter of course, which he did, and he said, "No, the engine oil is spot on the mark."

I tried to sound very concerned, and he said, "Don't worry. This old girl's due to go last month, and this was the last trip."

He took it away, and I got my new truck!

Every day we went swimming in the sea at Kyrenia, which we all found very nice We started work at seven o'clock in the morning, and finished work at twelve o'clock, because of the heat. It was my job to take the swimming truck loaded with chaps and bound for Kyrenia. The roads were very narrow, and this one twisted round the mountain pass. If we met a vehicle coming the other way, it was the one that kept his nerve the longest who managed to stay on the tarmac, and that one was usually me. You see, I didn't own the lorry, but I thought I'd always paid my taxes and dues, so I didn't care if I damaged it. Very bad, wasn't I?

One day, going over the mountains, we came to a sharp bend, where every large vehicle had to make two shunts in order to get round. I don't know why, but all the lads started their usual chant of "bet you can't do this in one."

"Well," I thought, "I've got to do it one day, and it might as well be now." There was no guard rail or fence alongside. The only thing that was there was an 800-foot drop, straight down to the valley below. About 20 chaps were in the back of the truck singing and shouting. I changed down a gear, put my hand between the two spokes in the steering wheel, and wound frantically with all my strength. All the lads fell silent while I executed this manoeuvre. After we straightened up, they all cheered. I was quite big-headed about it, but after a little while, my heart began to pound, as I realised what a risk I had taken. When we got back to camp, it was the talk of the camp, but if an NCO asked me, I denied it, because they would have put me on a charge.

When we went swimming at Kyrenia, there were no rocks or diving boards, so we had a good idea. The beach shelved down gradually, so I drove the lorry into the sea, and we got a lot more enjoyment diving off the back of it. After a few weeks of this, the salt water started to take its toll on the metal, eating away at the door panels. I had to do something quickly.

They were doing some building work on the camp and had plenty of sand and cement, so I stuffed paper and cardboard into the holes, mixed up the cement and trowelled it in and shaped it up. It looked good, so I got the Army paint and painted several coats. It looked even better, but I overlooked one thing, and that was the weight of the doors. When you opened the door, it almost knocked you over. Fortunately, this happened just before I was due to be demobbed, and I got away with it, because they did not do a detailed check of the lorry until I had gone.

The other thing I didn't like out there were the flies. They were awful. I noticed there were some large lizards in the wild. They used to get into buildings. Guess what? No flies. The lizards were catching them. This gave me the idea of making a pet of a lizard, so I found a young one and put it into a cardboard box with some bedding. Then I caught his favourite meals, which were large beetles, flies and crickets. Well, I housed him under my bed and soon he had free range of our large tent. There were six of us in the tent and always there were flies. After a while we all agreed that the fly population had dropped. We looked after him well, and handed him on to our successors when we left.

One day, I was taking the married men back to their homes around Nicosia. It was the same every day, at the same time. This particular day, I was slightly early. I was on my way to the last married man's house when I came across workmen digging up the road. Taken that the road was narrow, I had to pull over onto the scrub ground alongside the road. I reached the last house and had my customary cup of tea. Then I set of back to Nicosia and the camp. I didn't take much notice, but the workmen had gone and the trench was filled in.

What I didn't know was that the 'workmen' had planted a bomb in the trench. The track on the Bedford RL was wider at the front than the back, so the front wheels must have just missed this bomb, but the back wheels hit it, and with a loud explosion the back of the truck shot up in the air. I hit the roof with my head, and came back down and landed on the handbrake, breaking the little bone at the base of my spine. The pain was excruciating, and I can remember tears running down my face as my foot landed on the accelerator pedal.

The town of Nicosia was surrounded by a wall (it was called the Walled City). It had a road circling the wall and it was knocking-off time for the local workers. They all seemed to have bicycles. They were all over the road. They must have heard me coming because they scattered, many falling off their bikes.

I headed towards our camp on the Troodos road at break-neck speed and was stopped by the military police for erratic driving and speeding. They ordered me out of my cab and I refused because I was in such pain. This big Barbary sergeant was going to sling me in jail straight away, so I told him, "Look at the back of the truck," because he would not believe I had been blown up. He went round the back and saw the tailgate twisted and holed, and the rear axle with a hole and all its oil lost. He called up on the radio and got an ambulance and they transported me to BMH, British Military Hospital.

I thought I could play on this and spend an enjoyable time with the lovely nurses. But alas, when I got there, I felt better already, because the nurses were real battleaxes, and looked like our sergeant. I became remarkably fit after a few days, and asked to come out. When I did come out I went to inspect my truck, and there waiting for me, was another new one, so I didn't complain!

Going through two years in the Army was the worst thing in my life and when it was over it was like having everything one ever wanted. You see, it introduced me to smoking, which I have always regretted, and I hated guns and the injustice that was handed out. Looking back, it makes me feel as if we were all treated like animals.

Never mind, it was the time to leave and start living again. We went home on leave for a week. Then we had to return to Windsor and hand in all our kit. Dad lent me the Wolseley. She was a large black car, highly polished. When I drew up at the gates of the barracks, I got the full treatment as a visiting general. I saw straight away that I could take advantage of this.

I winked at the guardsman on the gate, and he realised what was happening, and went along with it. He shouted into the guardroom "officer waiting" and the corporal of horse had to turn out with the guardsmen on duty that morning. They formed a line and stood to attention whilst he opened the gate. I glided through very slowly, while the corporal of horse stood to attention and saluted me. I thought at the time, "If only they knew." It was a treat to be dressed in civvy clothes, and to be saluted was a good tale to tell all my friends.

We all hatched an idea, and milked it as much as we could. I loaded four of my friends into the car and drove all around the camp, getting salutes from all the NCOs and officers. Then it was time to leave, so I said goodbye to all my mates. I drove to the main gate and stopped at the guardroom and went inside to book out for the Very Last Time. It was a wonderful feeling. The corporal of horse felt really foolish and said that if he had known that I was an ordinary bloke he would have put me on a charge.

I said, "You missed your chance then, and you know what you can do with your charges," and with that I slouched out of the guardroom with hands in pockets, a real chargeable offence. Then home. BACK TO CLEEVE HILL.

9

Back Home

While I had been away, John and Daphne had got married (I was best man) and now they had a little girl, Tina. She was gorgeous.

It felt so good to wake up to birds singing, rain falling, and a cool atmosphere. I had breakfast, and then to work in the garage. Of course I was very rusty, owing to my being away for two years. Never mind, I got stuck in.

The first job I did was to be sent over to Postlip Lodge near Winchcombe, where I first met Mr Justice Ensor, a television judge. He had a little Morris 1000 that wouldn't start. I drew up outside his house. He came out and asked, "Who are you?"

I explained that I was John's brother at the garage, come to start the car. I thought, "He looks just the same as he did on the television," though in those days the picture was black and white. I suppose I didn't know what to expect, but as time went on we became friends.

While I was fixing his car, he came out with a full English breakfast even with a white napkin. I don't think he knew that garage mechanics have oily hands. I said sorry several times about the oil, but he said, "Don't worry. It's my oil anyway and you are stealing it."

We had a problem job come in one day. Every time the customer turned the car to the right or left there was a whirring sound. He was very concerned, thinking it might be something serious. He had been to several other garages with no result, so he tried us. The sound appeared to come from the rear area of the car.

We set to, and stripped out the boot - carpet, all the tools, the spare wheel, even the fuel tank. We painstakingly reassembled it all meticulously, and he took it home.

Next day he was back. The noise was still there. This time we suggested the rear suspension. We took it completely to pieces, checked everything thoroughly, greased all the nuts, bolts and pivots, which shouldn't have been necessary, and reassembled it. Off he went, and next day, there he was again, with the same whirring noise.

In desperation, I suggested I should sit in the back seat, slightly at an angle, while he drove round the block. I put my left arm over the back rest to support myself round the corners, and my fingers were curled round the shape of the back, and resting on the parcel shelf.

We negotiated the first bend at about 30 mph. The noise started up again, and all of a sudden something hit my fingers, and the noise stopped. I tried to retrieve whatever it was, but could not get hold of it as it was tucked back under the upholstery. We went back to the garage.

My brother said, "Hold on, let's get a mirror and see if we can retrieve it." You can imagine our surprise when we hooked it out with a piece of welding wire and found that it was a child's toy Dinky car, which was rolling back and forth, causing all the trouble. I said to the owner, "I've heard of a spare tyre behind the back seat, but never a spare car." He laughed loudly. I don't know why, because he had a huge bill for all the work we had done, but he didn't complain.

It is very rare in the motor trade that everything goes smoothly when you are looking for a little squeak, rattle or whirring sound.

Another problem job we had was where, once again, a customer had been to several other garages with no result, trying to find out why his car engine would fade out doing 60 mph. He had already had a new fuel pump and new manifold gaskets. The carburettor had been removed, stripped and overhauled, all to no avail. We thought, "Oh my goodness, what chance have we of finding what is the matter."

John and I tried it down the road and sure enough, the engine faded at 60 mph, so back to the garage we came. We checked the points to see they were opening and closing correctly. We started it up and left it ticking over because we thought it may have been the fuel tank not venting properly. We checked all the fuel pipes to make sure they were not bent or leaking. The fuel pipe from the tank entered the fuel pump via a small tap. This had a small plunger, which cut the petrol off if necessary when it was in the down position.

Sometime in the past, a mechanic must have pulled it up only about half way, restricting the flow of petrol. In tinkering about, John absentmindedly pulled it up - and there was the solution. We were very proud to think a little garage had solved what the large garages had failed to find.

We had a customer who had a very big building business, and he had a very smart Jaguar Mk9. It was two-tone paintwork

- black and white. I'd driven this car many miles in the past, and I loved it, but alas it came in for a service, which I undertook.

It was almost lunchtime and Mr Hitchens rang up and asked me to take it over to his office at Barnwood, so I put a seat cover over the seat and set off. Things were fine until I reached the Shurdington Road, where I thought I would give it a good blast-out.

The car had been fitted with Town and Country rear tyres which gave good grip in the snow, but after a while the tread would wear away and so would the grip. These tyres had worn, so with my foot hard down on the accelerator, the speed built up very satisfyingly. She reached 100 mph, so I took my foot off and was starting to slow down, when in the distance a little Ford car was backing out of a private drive.

I instantly braked hard, and then the rear of the car started to overtake the front of the car. In fact, we were sliding along sideways. As this was happening I thought, "I'm dreaming this. It can't be real," but then I heard and felt the expensive CRASH! When I regained my senses, I realised the driver of the Ford had seen me and slammed the car into first gear and shot forward down his drive, so I missed him. I looked to my right and saw an old Hillman buried into the offside doors. This car belonged to four police cadets. They had tried to miss me by driving onto my side of the road, as I was on theirs at the time. However I had managed to cross back onto my side, so we met there, with disastrous consequences.

I couldn't get out of the driver's door, so I started to get out of the passenger's door. (It gets worse!) The car was automatic and was still in gear and the engine was on tick-over. I accidentally trod on the accelerator and shot forward, demolishing two beautiful French-polished gate posts.

I eventually got out and asked the owner of the gate posts if I could use his phone to ring the garage. He must have been stunned, because he didn't answer but showed me the way to the phone. There was a mirror in the hallway and I caught a glimpse of my face - it was dripping with blood. This is what stunned him, I'm sure, not his gate posts.

When I got back to the scene of the crash, some people were laying one of the cadets out on the side of the road. I thought I'd killed him. He sat up and I breathed a sigh of relief. By that time Mr Plod came and took some measurements, and then started to grill me. At that time I was a Special police-man. Sounds good, but it's not really. Mr Plod demanded that I answer his questions. I refused, saying I was too shaken up. He got quite nasty, until I told him I was a Special Plod. Then he said, "OK, take all your papers into Winchcombe Police Station and let them deal with it."

Well, my father and brother came out in the breakdown truck and suspended the old Hillman to the back of the truck. John managed to close the nearside front door and drive the Jag back to the garage. I arrived half an hour later with the breakdown truck and the old Hillman, which went to the graveyard in the sky. It was a complete write-off. Dad made me ring Mr Hitchens and report the crash. I expected him to go ballistic, but all he said was, "Are you OK? The car can be repaired." What a relief.

John and I inspected the Jag. He opened the driver's door as I opened the rear door, and the whole side of the car fell out. The repair took many hours to complete. The most worrying part was the wooden dashboard, which was veneered. After we removed the dash, we had a word with a customer who was a very skilled carpenter. His name was Udelhoven, and he lived in a village near Winchcombe, called Gretton. He made a perfect job of it, one couldn't see any of his repairs.

We finished the job and phoned Mr Hitchens to say the car was ready. He came along and inspected our work and said he couldn't believe how we had repaired and repainted it so beautifully. John and I were pleased as well, except Dad, who kept on moaning something about losing his no claims on his insurance. I don't think he could take a little joke!

A friend who lived on Cleeve Hill, asked me if I would like to go on holiday with him, driving down to Italy in his Jaguar XK150. The only thing it wouldn't pass was a filling station. The family agreed to this reluctantly, so Mother got loads of food for us to take, including tins and tins of Ambrosia creamed rice.

We drove down to Paris and traffic was so quiet in those days, that we were looking out for British cars and waving to them. We had a little look round and carried on down to the Simplon Pass. It was beautiful scenery, but a bit scary when we came to a waterfall, which was cascading over the road and we went underneath it. Of course, the bends were hairpin, and it was a bit galling to be overtaken by little Citroen Deux Chevaux, which seemed to cling to the road like glue. Where we were braking on corners, they seemed to accelerate, and lean right over. We made our way down to Alassio in Italy, where we had a nice relaxing holiday.

Unfortunately cash ran rather short, and on the way back the fuel gauge was showing very low, and a warning light kept on flashing. We tried to lighten the car as much as possible, and ended up throwing most of the Ambrosia into the River Seine.

We arrived at the ferry and got on all right late at night. We tried to drive off in Dover, but there was an incline, and the petrol drained to the back, so we had to push the car and turn it round and go up in reverse. At the first roundabout we came to, we thought we were still in France, and went round it the wrong way. Fortunately, it was the early hours, and there was no traffic about.

We continued driving and I said to my friend, "Do you find that the car doesn't seem quite right in its handling?"

He said, "I think it's all right," so I didn't think any more of it, but when we arrived home we found the tyre on the rear was completely ruined, flat as a pancake. We must have driven miles on a flat tyre, but we made it home.

There was a girl who used to drive into Cheltenham each evening to pick up her sister from work. I can only describe her as a girl racer, road hog, a low-flying pilot, as she came over Cleeve Hill like a woman possessed. She impressed me very much! There was a bend in the road in front of the garage and she would come around that at full tilt, tyres screaming, the car leant to one side. She was gone in two seconds, so I couldn't get a good look at her.

Her father was a customer at the garage, and she and her sister Diana, and Joy Gillett, were the only girls who could drive in Winchcombe. If anyone said they had a problem with a car, she always said it was "dirt in the jets." She would always say that, even if a wheel fell off.

One day she brought her car into the garage for a job to be done. My mother called down to the garage, "Mike, can you take Miss Thompson back home to Winchcombe?"

You see, I didn't have a girlfriend, so Mum was determined to fix me up, or stitch me up, one or the other. Anyway, I took her home in our car and on the way, I don't know how I managed to pluck up courage, but I asked her to come out with her sister and a friend of mine. I went all numb when she said yes.

So, a couple of days later, I picked her and her sister and my friend up, in Dad's new Ford Zephyr. We proceeded into Cheltenham to see a film at the cinema. I knew a yard nearby where we could park. It belonged to one of our suppliers, so, out to impress the girls, I swept into the yard and headed for the far wall with the intention of stopping an inch or so from it, and letting the car stand there rocking gently. However, you've guessed it, I left it a moment too late, and hit the wall. Years later, I asked Pat what she thought of it, and she said, "I thought you were a big twit." Was my face red all evening!

Some time later I managed to get a radio for her from a written off car, so I asked her to bring her car in so I could fit it. I wanted it to look as if the radio had been fitted at the factory, so care was taken, until I came to drill some holes in the body work.

I was trying to impress Pat whilst she was looking on. I drilled the first hole through the bulkhead panel OK, then proceeded to drill the other hole, when all of a sudden, the drill went through the metal. I pulled the drill out, and as I did, battery acid cascaded out all over the carpets. I forgot the battery was just in line with the radio, so Pat put her finger over the hole, while I removed the battery. Then I had to wash the carpets with cold water. That done, I had to repair the battery. As luck would have it a tubeless tyre plug just fitted, so all was fine again. I refilled the battery and wired up the radio. Pat turned it on and it worked well. I think it was left in the car until it was traded in. The next time she came belting past the garage, I could see her mouth singing away with the music.

One day, I bought Pat a black miniature poodle puppy called Mitzi. When Pat took her home, her mother said, "You're not keeping it here. Take it back after you have had your lunch."

Well Mitzi had that look that makes one wilt and by the time Pat had finished her lunch, Mitzi had graciously accepted a bowl of milk, and Pat's mother had fallen for her. She stayed - even after we got married Pat had to leave her behind, as her mother could not bear to be parted from Mitzi. Whenever we went to visit, Mitzi was laying on her father's lap in the big armchair. She owned the place now.

While Mitzi was still a puppy I managed to get a day off and we went to Weymouth, and took Mitzi for a walk along the Chezil Beach. This is a long spit of land, made up of pebbles thrown up by the sea. Mitzi ran down to examine the waves, while we frantically called her back, as they were quite high and she was almost swept out to sea. Thank goodness she responded, and came out quickly. Pat's mother would never have forgiven us. We kept her securely on the lead after that.

The first car I owned was a little Austin A30, which wasn't really my image because it was powder-blue, but I was quite proud of it. I customised it with flasher indicators instead of semaphore arms (which were always jamming), a radio, an interior mirror with a small clock in it, and best of all a go-faster red stripe along both sides of the car.

One night I decided to take a mate out to show off a little. We did a round robin trip, which took us through a village called Bredon. After going through the village, I put my foot down and was looking and talking to my friend, when all of a sudden he shouted, "Look out!" It was too late to brake. I looked up to see a very sharp left-hand bend.

All I could do was turn the steering wheel hard. I thought we were going to turn over any time now. Thank goodness it didn't. This was a bragging point. "Just like going round on rails," I said. I don't think my friend agreed with me, as his face had turned ashen and he didn't speak for a while.

In those days cars were quite small compared with today's cars. When I see an older car of the same vintage, I wonder how four people managed to get in, let alone sit down. With four people in the car, every slight incline meant I had to change down several gears and we crawled along. In fact I was overtaken by a pushbike on one occasion. That was the end. I had to sell it and start using the firm's cars.

That wasn't the end of the A30, as the new owner wanted her geed up, so he gave us the job of fitting a brand new MG Midget engine and gearbox, which didn't take much work to convert. The new engine came with two carburettors. What with the new 1098 cc motor, it went like stink. I only wished I could have afforded to do it.

I was left driving a Hillman Minx with the springs sticking through the seats. Pat used it one day and came to pick me up from work. On the way up Cleeve Hill she spotted me walking down and stopped to pick me up. On starting up again, she let out the clutch, and the exhaust promptly fell off! We had got married by then, and consequently had no money at all.

At the garage, we looked after a horsebox for a racehorse trainer. His name was Bill Marshall, and his three sons were called Tom, Dick and Harry. The horsebox was a Ford Thames V8. The usual reason for breaking down was getting the electrical distributor wet. Whenever someone topped up the radiator and spilled a drop of water, it always went over the distributor and then the vehicle would not start. Drying it out was not easy, especially when it was raining, because the distributor was situated at the bottom of the engine and right at the front. The radiator was fitted very close to it, and we only had about two inches of space to work in. What with having to lay down on the road in flowing water, it was no joke.

I had an idea one day, and that was to tip some meths over the distributor and set fire to it. This should dry everything out, so I tried it. It worked very well, except for one thing - it burned the plug leads, so that was no good, plus I got a telling-off from John. He said, "You fool. You could have set fire to the whole lot."

Upon reflection, I realised it was rather stupid, but with all the trouble we had with that horsebox, later on he said it was a pity I didn't set fire to it, because it was such a pain.

A few months later, the driver blew the engine up, so we took the opportunity of selling Bill Marshall the latest four-cylinder (Cost Cutter) petrol engine. Ford Motors had made a conversion kit for it, but the sting came straight away. Mr Marshall wanted it in and running by the next day, as they had a horse running at Newmarket racecourse.

We started work outside in the yard that very night. We worked all night and had it running by 6.30 am. We were both worn out, but we still had to road test it and run it in for a few miles, so we drove it to Northleach and back. We handed it to the driver at eight o'clock, went and had some food and then started our other work for that day. All day we were living on tenterhooks, until we heard it coming up the hill. What a relief! The driver said it ran like a dream. I think they had a winner as well!

We had a contract with Cheltenham police to attend car accidents and tow the cars into the garage to be, we hoped, repaired. Some of them were write-offs.

We had a call one night from the police to retrieve a new Jaguar 2.4, which had wedged itself on its side between two big trees. It was nicely dented all over, so it didn't matter if we put more dents in it. We got it out and back to the garage.

The insurance company came and inspected it and said, "Get on and fit a complete new body shell." That was a huge big job. The new body shell had to be prepared and painted, and then we had to strip out the old one, and build up all the parts into the new. We had the car for about four months in all. John did about 70% of the work, as I had to do the other jobs that came in.

When the car was finished, we had to deliver it back to the customer, who lived in Tunbridge Wells. There were no motorways in those days, so it was a very long way. We received a lovely letter from the owner, saying it was just like new again.

We had quite a few cars to deliver back to different customers. One time, Pat and I were going out for the evening, but that was scrapped by John, who told us to drive a car to RAF Gaydon, also a long way off. We protested a lot, but in the end we had to go.

When we got there it was late. John had instructed us to get the satisfaction note signed and not to come away without it. We asked the guard commander if he could locate the man who owned the car. It was getting later and later, and eventually he returned and said the man couldn't be found, so I said to Pat, "Well we can't take the car all the way back to the garage." So we left the keys with the guard commander with strict instructions to get the man to sign the paper and send it back to us.

When we got back home, John went mad, but it was midnight by now and we were fed up, so we went off home, and a couple of days later the satisfaction note came in the post, so all ended up OK.

In conjunction with the police call-out arrangement, we also ran a night breakdown service. One cold night, we got a call from a young man who said he had broken down right out in the country and didn't know what to do. He was able to give us directions to where he was waiting, and I set off.

It was literally freezing and as I set out, high on the Cotswolds, my lights picked out an object on the road. It seemed to move, so I stopped and got out to investigate. It turned out to be a pigeon, whose feet had become frozen to the road. He looked so frightened, that I set about helping him. I held my hands over his feet, and eventually the warmth thawed them out, and I was able to pick him up. He did not seem to be injured in any way and was soon able to fly off.

I continued on my way to the breakdown, colder than ever, as the heater was not working. To my amazement I found the man was actually at his mother's home, nice and warm. He had called me out so that he would have a workable car to use in the morning. You can imagine how I felt. I did the repair, but I charged him several times the going rate, and left him well aware that I thought him a spoiled brat.

Our garage was built on the side of Cleeve Hill, on a steep slope. The petrol sales and the office were level with the road, but the workshop and yard were below them. Below these, was a strip of garden about 15 yards wide by 60 yards long. The boundary along the garden was a Cotswold stone wall, and behind that was a field.

We were crying out for a flat surface for parking, so Dad arranged for builders and council workers to dump their spoil over the edge down into the garden. Underneath this spoil were old cars, car body shells, etc. In fact lorries came from all over to dump top soil etc. After a few months, it started to look very good. The top was coming up level with the yard and we were pleased to have more parking space.

One fateful day, it started raining very heavily and continuously. It lasted all day and night - constant heavy rain. We all went to bed, but next morning we were devastated because the soil had slipped and the whole top half of the hillside slid down about 50 yards into the field, carrying the lovely Cotswold stone boundary wall, which was about 20 yards long, with it. That was all we wanted, because we did not have much money. We had to employ two brothers who were dry-stone wallers to rebuild the wall back on the boundary with a decent foundation. It took them about two weeks of solid work, with my brother and I helping as much as we could along with our other work. They made a beautiful job of it.

My father had to go and explain to the farmer who owned the field what had happened. He said, "Well, I don't use it for arable, just grazing occasionally, so it does not matter about the newly formed hillocks which have got pushed up." So he was very good about it.

A few yards lower down the Cleeve Hill road, there was a small church with a corrugated iron roof. We called it "the tin tabernacle." On Sundays we got fed up with it, because its adherents used to park their cars all along the road, interfering with our car parking, hence the reason we were trying to increase our own parking area. Of course, we had to work on Sundays to make a living.

One early morning in summer, about dawn, I could not sleep, so I decided to walk from the garage, across Cleeve Common to Nutters Wood.

It was very hot and still. It was a sheer delight, because the dawn chorus started, and it was a wonderful cacophony of sound, as they competed to see who could sing the loudest. It was just like being back on the farm. There were no sounds from the road. It was quiet, except for the birds.

The animals that I saw were rabbits, squirrels, a couple of weasels and a stoat, a fox and clouds of butterflies. I didn't get as far as I intended, and on the way back there were two skylarks singing away and getting higher and higher.

My eyes were drawn to the view across the valley to the Malvern Hills in the distance. I have never seen anything so beautiful as on that particular day. I should have realised that, as it was so clear, rain was on the way, and by lunchtime, it was really raining heavily.

The other phenomenon that I marvelled at was in the autumn, when the colder weather was coming. Fog was rolling over and over down into the valley, while we had gorgeous sunshine on the hill. Down in the valley you could not see your hand before your face the fog was so thick, and freezing.

About now, even though we had tried to extend the garage with our earth moving efforts, it was proving too small, and we began to consider selling up and moving elsewhere. Mum and Dad had always wanted to live on the South coast, and they found a garage in Barton-on-Sea, a few miles east of Bournemouth. It had a car agency and showroom, quite big workshops and even a small grocery shop, with a flat above it. They liked it and bought it.

I have never resented anything as much as those two years I wasted doing National Service. I can't say I gained anything at all by it, and neither did most of the rest of us. Oh, it is true that those who went in as Teddy Boys or yobs came out smarter and more disciplined, and a few enjoyed the comradeship and the regulated lifestyle. But for most of us it was two years stolen from us.

As for me, I don't think life was ever quite the same. I learned that so-called comrades would lose their kit and steal yours without a thought, that those in authority were either bullies in the case of most of the sergeants, or spoiled ignoramuses in the case of most of the officers.

My relationship with my family was never quite the same as before. My father never went into the Army during the war, because farmers were exempt. My brother never did National Service because his rebuilt arm meant he was medically unfit. They never really accepted that I had no choice and they looked upon it as a two-year holiday. While I was away the four of them had worked together at Cleeve Hill, and although they welcomed me back, I always felt the odd one out, so when they announced the move I was not altogether surprised. It was time to go independent.

Pat and I decided to stay in Cheltenham. We had started buying a bungalow, and we had a little girl of six months now, Andrea. We were a family and I had something of my own to work for, so when the others moved out, I stayed on to help the new owner - my employer.

He was not a man to get his hands dirty, and liked to stay in the office - hardly practical in a small business - so the work was done by me, and he even employed a mechanic to sell the petrol. I insisted on this man coming down into the workshop, as there was too much work for one. The boss got me working Sundays as well, and had a girl working weekends on the petrol pumps. She was useless, and I spent more time running up and down sorting out accounts for her, than actually working on cars.

One winter's evening it looked very much like snow, so he got me to take the breakdown truck home, in case of a call-out that night. Next morning, sure enough, it had snowed heavily, blocking the road to the garage. I knew there was a gateway in this field, so, like a fool, I said, "I can get there. This vehicle is a four-wheel drive."

It wasn't until I got to the garage in the snow that I realised what a fool I was - I could have had a day at home, like everyone else, including the boss. It was the final straw, so considering the low wages I was on, I left.

My family asked me to join them at the New Milton garage. I decided to go, but it was a bit difficult. Pat was pregnant with Michele, and Andrea was only about 18 months old, so house hunting and moving would be very difficult.

We decided that I would go and stay with my parents, see how things worked out, and travel home each weekend. This worked out OK. I rang up each day, and one day I asked Pat how she was, and she said, "OK, but I've got the backache."

When I told my mother this, she said, "You go home straight away, Mike. That baby will soon be on the way."

Sure enough, a few hours after I got home, I was being bossed about by the nurse, and helped to deliver Michele at home. Now we had two dear little girls. I was so thrilled. I took them out in the pram and, being rather inexpert at getting it up and down the pavement, pushed it in the middle of the road. A car soon stopped and the driver shouted, "What are you doing in the road with a pram?"

I said, "I've as much right to be in the road with my pram, as you have with your car."

He drove off, rather bemused.

Andrea and Michele grew up to be lovely girls and are the apple of my eye.

10

Self-Employment

It didn't work out down at New Milton, so I returned to Cheltenham.

I got a job at another small garage, nearer town. It was a family firm. The father was a town councillor, and he was rarely there. His son only wanted to do taxi work and serve petrol. There again, I was on my own in the workshop, as well as serving petrol when he was out. I could see no future in it, so I started doing repairs on my drive. The neighbours didn't seem to mind, not even when the Duckhams tanker delivered bulk oil!

When I had built up a good clientele, I looked out for some premises. A carpenter friend told me of some he had recently vacated. There was just room to get two cars in, and it had the added facility of a pit. Pat did not expect me to last long at it, and bought a little notebook to keep the accounts in. She put 'sales' one end and 'purchases' the other, and expected me to give up before they met in the middle!

When Pat was 17 and had just passed her driving test, she and her family went on holiday to a hotel in Bournemouth.

Whilst there, her father was taken ill and was unable to drive them home.

The only way to do it was to allow Pat to drive - an opportunity right up her street! There were no motorways in those days and the car was a big Jaguar. The hotel manager was astounded that this was going to be attempted. "Is that little girl going to drive that great car?" he said.

When they set off, all the hotel staff came out to see them off. I am telling you this to explain that after we were married we generally took her parents on holiday with us, as her mother considered her father too old now for them to be going on their own.

In 1966 we were on holiday with them in Brixham, having a very happy time playing with our two little girls, Andrea and Michele, when the police came looking for us with devastating news. My mother had committed suicide. We knew she had been suffering from depression. She had retired from the garage and they had bought a nice bungalow in Walkford, not far away. She was always an extremely hard worker and probably missed it all. Who knows? Everyone blames themselves and has various theories when there is a suicide, especially by a much-loved mother. We cut the holiday short and came home, of course. The day of the funeral was so sad. She now lies in Highcliffe cemetery.

To our amazement, Father remarried within the year and left the business for John and Daphne to run. We kept up a loose contact with him, but they moved house so often, usually every two years, that it was difficult. They lived in Ringwood three times, Stonehouse three times, Gloucester, Boston, Grantham, and Skegness twice, plus some others.

To return to the garage trade, one day, we had a smashed car brought in - a Vauxhall Cresta. It was owned by a horse-racing correspondent, and he said, "Get on and do the job, no matter how much it costs."

I thought this job would set me up and get a little capital behind me. I worked day and night until it was repainted and looked beautiful. When I rang him and told him it was ready, he told me to get the bill ready. I think it was a few hundred.

In those days, all garages gave customers credit. He paid a small amount when he picked up the car, and we never saw him again! That was a shock to us, but we live and learn.

I was working very successfully, when a council official paid me a call and said, "What are you doing here?"

I said, "Mechanics."

He said, "You can't do any more work here because you haven't got planning permission."

I explained there was a pit in the workshop, so it must have been a garage before, but he said, "You won't get planning permission. You'll have to get out."

This was a bombshell, as I had the two little girls by now. However, Pat's sister, Diana, was working in the Planning Office at the Municipal Offices. A large woodworking factory in the middle of Cheltenham had burnt down, and the Council had just decided to split it up into small business units and rent them out. She passed this information on to us, and I was soon signing a five-year lease for the first one.

The next month, the Council decided not to follow this plan, but to demolish it and make a car park of it. However, as I had already signed, they had to leave my bit standing and make the car park round it. I built up a really good business in these premises, and we saved every penny we could over those five years in the hope of buying our own premises one day and say goodbye to paying rent.

It was a long, tall building and extremely convenient for getting parts from suppliers, etc. Also customers could walk into town and do their shopping while their cars were repaired, etc. The only inconvenience was parking, as usual.

I took on a German mechanic to help me. He was an excellent mechanic, and also taught me some German words - most of them unsuitable, but I still remember one - 'schraubenzieher' meaning screwdriver.

One day a customer brought in a Jaguar 3.4 (like Morse's car), saying there was a smell of petrol. I was working on another car at the time, so I did not get on with it immediately. The petrol leak must have dripped onto the starter motor, and as soon as I pressed the starter, there was a whoosh, and it went up in flames. We used every fire extinguisher we had, but it made no difference, so, worried that everything in the workshop would catch fire, we pushed it out into the road and rang the fire brigade.

When they came, they tackled the fire with great enthusiasm. You would have thought it was a huge building on fire instead of a small car. They attacked the lovely veneered dashboard with an axe, and completely destroyed it. They said there could have been smouldering behind it. I don't know how, as the car was swimming in water - they just enjoyed wrecking it. If they hadn't attacked the dashboard and its instruments, it would not have been a write-off. The customer was very abusive, but it was hardly my fault - I hadn't even worked on it. I had only jumped into it to start it.

I found out later that he had only just bought it from an auction and had not even had someone to look over it. He was lucky it had not happened in his garage at home. I left him to sort it out with the previous owner, and his insurance company.

I used to maintain the vehicles for a fashion firm called Peter Richards. They had about 45 shops all over England. Their vans were beautifully lined inside with veneered wood to protect the dresses they carried. Unfortunately, these big vans had a tendency to keep breaking down, due to incompetence by their drivers.

One evening one of them broke down near Derby. Not knowing what the fault was, and because the driver had already left it and was on his way home by train, I loaded up tools and a few spares into my old breakdown van. I admit this was not exactly clean in the back, due to oil and grease.

I set off from Cheltenham at 6 pm and arrived at the broken down van around 8 pm. It was pitch-dark so I removed the engine cowlings and tried to start it. It was a diesel engine and one of the special metal pipes to the injectors had fractured. Of course I had not got a new one, and could not get one, so I thought the best thing to do was to unload the van of its dresses and gowns, and load them into my oily one. I locked up the gowns van (as they called it) and came back to Cheltenham loaded to the roof.

I parked the breakdown van on my drive and next morning I pulled up at the warehouse in Charlton Kings and explained my predicament of the night before to the firm's accountant. He was not very happy and neither was I. The staff unloaded my van and I departed for another day's work.

Meanwhile I got some spares together and went back out that evening to Derby with a friend of mine who worked for Dowty's during the day. We fitted the new parts, bled the diesel system, turned the key and away she went.

I sat my friend in the driver's seat and said to him, "OK off you go." I saw panic set in on his face.

"I've never driven a big thing like this," he said, "especially at night."

So I said, "Well here's your opportunity to drive a big vehicle."

We started off nice and slowly. After a while he became more confident. When we got back to the garage he was all smiles and rather cock-a-hoop at his achievement.

Quite a lot of Americans were living in Cheltenham at that time. They were sent over here for three years at a time to work at GCHQ, the listening post. They brought their families, invariably their furniture, and of course their cars. Once here, they needed their cars maintained.

One or two had heard that I did Jags and other big cars, and as soon as I had done a few jobs for them, the word went round, and I had a lot of them as customers. Americans, of course, are very sociable and we became good friends.

One in particular was Billy Liner, a huge genial 20-stoner. I had some very amusing times with him and his pals. He smashed up his Chevrolet Camero, a super looking car (before!). The insurance company told him to take it to their designated repairers, who said it couldn't be repaired - it was a write-off.

He didn't stand for this, so he brought it round to me. I agreed to do it, so long as he located the parts in the States and got them over to me. He agreed, so I told the insurance company what was happening. They were more than pleased for him to go ahead.

The parts soon arrived from the States via their base at Upper Heyford, and then I got on with the job. I did this repair in good time - fortunately all the panels bolted on and off instead of welding. One part of the front chassis member was badly mangled. I knew it needed to go on a jig to be pulled back into shape, so I fixed it as best I could at the time, fitted all the panels and sprayed the front end. I fitted all new lamps and the bumper bar. A couple of holes would not line up because of the damage, so I took it down to my brother in New Milton, who at that time had a panel beating repair shop with a jig.

Boy, did this car go! I arrived early and we started straight away by putting it on the chassis jig. After about three hours everything was in line and all the measurements were spot-on, to manufacturer's specifications. My brother then said he should road test it! He went out of the garage with rear wheels spinning, onto the main road. He went down the road and three or four minutes later we heard him coming back. It was like a flash of lightening as he passed us. Today at that speed we would be hung, drawn and quartered. When my brother came back his first words were, "Pretty docile! Job done."

Billy accepted the car back, and was very satisfied.

At that time I owned a speedboat - quite a nice-looking thing, but rather under-powered.

I invited a couple of friends plus Billy for a trip up the river from Bredon, near Tewkesbury. It was a lovely day, but I was nervous about putting it into the river off the trailer. Still, it went OK. We all got in and sat down. I started the engine and off we went up the river.

I couldn't help noticing that I was having trouble seeing over the front of the boat. It seemed rather high. I looked over my shoulder at my passengers. They seemed a bit low down, and then I noticed they were ankle-deep in water. It was then

I realised I had not put the bilge plugs into the bottom of the boat. We were gradually filling up with water!

I aimed for the nearest bank and we disembarked - hurriedly. I fitted the bilge plugs by plunging my arm into the deepening water and finding the holes they fitted into. There were a lot of snide remarks and wisecracks, but I rose above them all. I started the engine and managed to pump the water out of the boat, and the rest of the trip was uneventful.

Undeterred, the same group of us decided to go on a fishing trip up the River Severn. We arrived at the slipway to launch the boat. We got our kit together, while the boat was moored up, and loaded it in.

Billy, of course, had to outdo us by loading up a huge coffin-like box, which took up 90% of the floor space. We were all pulling his leg about this, and making witty remarks. He opened it up and showed us inside. I swear his equipment could have caught anything from a minnow to a huge whale. The remaining floor space was taken over by booze. It was American beer, American whisky, gin, brandy, Bacardi and other drinks that I didn't know. They weren't just ordinary bottles - they were half gallons and gallons. He had a special net that he put the beer into, tied it onto the boat, and then dropped it into the water to keep it nice and cool.

Well, we anchored up near a village, and there we sat, pretending to catch fish, but really the booze took over. We were all pie-eyed and three parts cut. You can imagine a hot day, with us sitting in the boat with no shade, what this drink was doing to us.

The fishing lines had been out in the water for at least a couple of hours. Nobody cared if we caught a fish or not, but then a shout came, "Your line's moving." It was hauled in and on the end was a decent sized fish. None of us, except Billy, was a fisherman, so we didn't know what make it was. Billy insisted on keeping it, and taking it home to eat. None of us fancied it. Just for a laugh, Billy threw the line in again with some different bait on it, and left it. Blow me, within a couple of minutes he had caught another one, about the same size.

We were all like little schoolboys, laughing and joking, but it started to get late, so we decided we had had enough. We managed to get back to the slipway. We disembarked and I had to back the boat trailer down the slipway into the water. It took me six or seven goes at reversing to get it somewhere in line so that we could float the boat on. This became a real circus. We were all laughing hysterically, especially when the boat would not go on forwards - we got it crossways. The more we tried, the more it became hilarious.

People who were waiting and looking on joined in as well. The more they laughed, the more we laughed and we became weaker and weaker. We managed to get the boat lined up, and then pulled with all our might, and got the boat on the trailer, but tilted at an angle. The fish were slopping about in the boat, causing more laughter.

We all bundled into the car and drove back to Cheltenham. To our amazement the fish were still there, flopping about in the boat. Billy went round the neighbours asking how to cook them. No one knew. He decided to take them home with him and ask his wife, Alice. We heard that she sent him off with a flea in his ear (or perhaps a fish). They were beginning to get a bit smelly in the heat, so they ended up in his dog. He must have been ravenous!

Billy was so grateful (!) for these outings, that he decided to arrange one of his own. He booked up for us to go shark fishing in Looe, Cornwall.

There were five of us, all disreputable. He had booked a trip on a boat, and I decided to take my speedboat too, so that we could fill the time in while waiting. It was loaded up with camping equipment, fishing equipment, mainly Billy's, and food. We started off down the motorway, very merry, with two other cars in tandem. The journey was uneventful.

We reached the campsite, which was a farmer's field, with no facilities. We had to go down to the town first thing in the morning and last thing at night! I digress.

We unloaded the boat and started to erect the tents. One of them was quite big, and fought back enthusiastically. There was a great deal of hysterical laughing because nothing seemed to fit until we found out we were trying to erect it the wrong way round. I should have taken my wife's advice, which is: "If all else fails, read the instructions."

Anyway, with the job completed, we decided to have a meal. Billy was a past master at cooking in the wild. First of all, he cut away a square of turf and set it aside. Then he got the charcoal and filled up the hole with it, and set it alight. After about ten minutes, he brought out a wire tray and loaded that with weiners, sausages, eggs and bacon, mushrooms, and tomatoes, and proceeded to make us a gorgeous meal. We all stuffed ourselves and sat round the fire telling jokes.

I had a camp bed and I have never felt so cold in my life, as the cold penetrated up from the earth, through the bed and into me. I had to get up at three o'clock, I was so cold. I didn't want to wake the others so I went for a walk across the fields, and looked at the sea. Of course, my previous experience of camping was two years under canvas in Cyprus where it was hot, so this was a bit of a shock. The other fellows brought a great big groundsheet and padded this and padded that, and they slept soundly all night, complaining of the heat in the

135

morning. As I returned from my walk, the cold night was soon forgotten, as Billy was cooking breakfast. In American tradition, the coffee pot went on first and was left on all day and all night, so a good time was had by all.

We all loaded into the cars and drove to Looe harbour, where we had to pick the boat up. What a shock we had! Billy had got the wrong week! We had to make our own amusement. Thank goodness I had brought the speed boat. We had a lovely time throwing it around on the sea, hitting the waves, taking off and flopping down the other side with a jolt.

This may have caused the outboard motor to conk out, so we managed to get it back into the harbour just as the tide was going out. We tied it up to a metal ring let into the harbour wall, but had to keep releasing the rope as the water level went down. I started to strip the engine down, but then the harbour master put in an appearance and said, "You can't park that there. You will have to move it to the top end moorings up the river."

We were at a loss to know how to get it there. When the tide had gone out there was just a little stream running through the middle of the harbour. Billy said that as he was already so wet, he would get out of the boat, take the rope, which was tied to it, and float the boat up the stream with him pulling it. We got out, climbed up onto the quay, and followed him along up above.

The summer crowds were milling about and looking for some entertainment, which they now got. Wisecracks were being thrown at Billy, which caused a lot of hilarity between us and the crowds. Billy certainly did look a sight. Imagine 20-stone plus wading up the stream, a fisherman's trilby on his head, getting deeper and deeper in the water until suddenly he disappeared down a hole, and his hat floated away. This didn't stop him, because he emerged up the other side of the hole, still with the boat in tow. People were literally rolling about on the ground, and some thought we were being invaded by a foreign force. When he came up the other side everyone clapped. Billy had not realised that he had lost his hat until he looked back and saw it still afloat about 20 yards away. He released the boat and scrabbled after it, going down into the deep water again. He realised that people were laughing at him, so he went under the water and came up underneath the hat, swivelled round, and swam up to the boat. There was another crescendo of clapping, wisecracks from us and then the crowd joined in with wisecracks. Eventually we got the boat moored and Billy came out of the water dripping.

We had to take him back to the campsite. He owned a Volkswagen Estate car. It had two exhaust pipes coming out of the back, and Billy opened the tailgate, sat just inside with his bare feet dangling in front of the hot exhaust, and was transported back to camp. He got changed and I started getting the meal ready, but we had run out of eggs. "No bother," we thought, "we will go to the farmer and get some more." One of our party said that he would go in his car.

When he got inside the farmer's gate, he was met by half a dozen geese. He told us that it was over 500 geese and they all attacked him! He came back without any eggs, so I said I would go. Sure enough, when I got there, there were geese, but by no stretch of the imagination were there 500. There were about half a dozen. They were honking and hissing at me, but I knew what geese were like, so I strode straight up to the front door with the geese trying to nip me, and the farmer came out and said, "I can tell you are from the country. Your mate isn't. He cleared that five-bar gate in a couple of seconds."

I explained to him that I was a farmer's son and that broke the ice, as he said, "Oh well, in that case you can have a dozen eggs free."

We reciprocated when we left and left him some wieners and sausages.

After the meal we decided to drown our sorrows by going to the pub in Looe. On the way back, we almost had an accident through a young fellow in his car driving out of a side turning without looking. We had to skid to a stop, and of course, this started the driver of our car taking off after him to remonstrate with him. The car chase really got going. We were going at breakneck speed through very narrow streets, trying not to lose sight of the car in front. It was dark at night, so we followed his rear lights, getting closer and closer, until he turned the lights off and disappeared.

We cruised around for a bit until we were stopped by the police. They said there had been complaints about two cars chasing each other. We pleaded complete ignorance, and promised we would let the police know if we saw them. Fortunately, we were all very pleasant and relaxed from being on holiday. We drove up to the campsite and I made sure I had something to lie on that was warmer.

Next day we packed up and came home, to be welcomed by our wives and families, with, "Where have you been? You're late."

On another occasion, we took the speedboat out on the river, only to discover, after we had pushed it out from the slipway into the middle, that someone somehow had forgotten the keys. I don't know who that was, but talk about being up the creek without a paddle - that was us. What a load of prats we must have looked, leaning over the sides of the boat paddling with our hands and getting nowhere.

At last we reached the shore. I was out of the boat and into the car, driving as fast as I could back to Cheltenham, to collect the keys from my house. Oh, drat it! Now I've told you who forgot the keys in the first place.

I drove back to the river and from then on everything went well. We made our way up to Strensham lock. It was Bill's turn to drive the boat, and as he weighed over 20 stone, when he sat down in the driving seat the boat listed to one side quite considerably. Bill thought he would do a figure of eight in a large basin of water we came to. It was fine going round the right-handed turn, but when he swung round the left-handed turn we were all drinking beer and laughing so much, we didn't notice water was flowing in over the side because of the weight of Billy. The first we knew of it was when our feet became wet and cold. Billy straightened up and we had to use the bilge pump again.

The River Severn has a nasty tendency to rise in height and although it was a beautiful day, it had rained very heavily three days before up in the Welsh Mountains. It takes water about three days to reach Tewkesbury, and it rose about six inches this day, so when we reached the slipway to go home, the jetty was surrounded by water. Bill said he would get on the jetty and guide the boat onto the trailer. I meantime reversed the trailer down the slipway, taking six or seven goes to line it up with the boat (I think we had all drunk a little too much beer on the trip).

Bill started to pull the boat with a rope, swaying and leaning out over the water, with the other two friends trying to manhandle the boat onto the trailer. All of a sudden there was a yell and all 20 stone of him lost his balance and he tried to jump towards dry land. He missed by about a yard and caused a tidal wave that drenched all of us except Bill. All he got was one wet foot.

Soon after this, most of the Americans were recalled to the

States, and I was sorry I would not see them again, especially Billy.

You may think by these last stories that I was always having a good time, but these days were few, because I had to build up my business.

Some of the cars were great big American gas-guzzlers. Several of them protruded about four feet over the front of the lift when I drove them on, and they just fitted widthways. Everything was big, hunky and heavy. I had to take an auto gearbox out of one to repair it. I was completely on my own, and didn't have the right equipment, so I had to improvise with jacks and wooden blocks. I let the gearbox down to chest height, and then panicked. The jacks wouldn't go any lower, so I took a deep breath and lifted it with super-human strength and walked with it to the workbench, where I almost collapsed.

Then my thoughts turned to what I would do when I had to refit the box to the car. I made up a wheeled platform, placed the gearbox on it and pushed it under the car. I connected two small but strong chains to the box and dropped the ramp down until it was about a foot above the gearbox. There was an inspection cover in the floor pan of the car about three inches wide, so I threaded the chains through it, opened the passenger door, and used the engine crane to lift the gearbox. I then bolted it into position.

Then I had a dreadful thought: would the gearbox work after all this, or would I have to go all through the process again? I finished refitting the gearbox with its components and finally refilled it with new auto box fluid. With trepidation, I turned the key. The engine started. So far, so good. Now came the moment of truth. I selected reverse gear, and the car moved backwards. I was so pleased.

Looking across to the workbench on the way out of the garage, I saw all the old worn parts, and hoped I hadn't forgotten anything. My worries were unfounded. As I drove out of the yard on road test, the gearbox changed up and down perfectly. After that I realised that you could do anything if you improvised.

I had to make, yes make, many special tools. The main agents would not help in any way, as they wanted the job for themselves. It was at the time that catalysts and fuel emissions were coming on to the scene. As I was doing the American cars that had all these things already, I had the manuals, so I became quite knowledgeable about the new innovations. One day, Bristol Street Motors phoned me asking for information on a fault that they had with fuel emissions. This was my chance.

I said, "Do you remember the times when I phoned you for advice, and do you remember what you said? You told me it was my fault for taking on the job."

"We wouldn't say a thing like that," he said, but I knew he remembered because he then said, "Did you fix it?"

I said, "Yes, no thanks to you, so why should I help you?"

I am not usually like this. I'll help everyone who wants advice, and by the way, Bristol Street Motors towed the problem car to my garage for me to fix, which I did.

In 1970 Neil was born. Need I say anything more? He was born at home, and I decided that while I was home for a few days, I would install a stereo record player. The noise was tremendous while I adjusted the speakers, but eventually it was done.

Neil had obviously inherited the mechanic's gene, because over the next couple of years he thoroughly demolished the whole thing. I don't know how many times I had to replace the stylus because he kept wrenching it off.

His grandfather thought the world of him. He was the only boy in the family for many years, and he wanted to teach him carpentry, etc. Unfortunately, Grandpa died when Neil was four years old, so he never really got to achieve his ambition.

Pat had to go and collect spares most weeks, as suppliers did not deliver very much in those days, so Neil had to go with her. He got very bored, sitting in the car one day, and demolished the heater system, then panicked, and got the manual out to see if he could repair it. He was expecting me to be very angry, but I admired him for trying to reassemble it. He was just the same with his bike, later on, and cost me a fortune in bicycle wheels. He was very accident-prone, and we spent quite a bit of time in Accident and Emergency.

Another American car I had to repair was a sports car called a Stingray. The owner had hit the front end of the car, and smashed the bodywork, which was made of fibreglass.

One could buy new panels in sections, so all the panels were ordered from the States. When they came, I started work and removed the bumper bar and side lamps and of course the head lamps, which were the 'pop-up' sort. I cut off all the damaged panels and cut the new panels to size and fibreglassed them to the existing panels.

When it was all done, I sprayed all the panels and then refitted the lamps, etc. The headlamps were operated by vacuum from the engine. It had two rubber vacuum pipes going from the headlamps back to the headlamp switches. Whilst fitting the rubber tubes, I inadvertently fitted them the wrong way round, so when the lights were switched on, one head lamp stayed down and the other hinged up, and vice versa. It looked as though the car was winking and I thought it rather funny, so I left it like that until the customer came to collect his car.

He said, after noticing the fault, "That's not right, you know."

I said, "Of course it is. It's so pleased to see you again, it's winking at you."

I was operating the light switch at the time. He saw the funny side of it, so I connected the pipes correctly and away he went, very happy.

The five-year lease I had on the Sherborne Place premises was soon due to end. I applied to have it extended, but they would only give me a year. That was no good, so we started looking round for other premises. We had saved hard and had some cash, but there was nothing available.

My brother was going to expand his business and open a panel-beating and spraying workshop on a trading estate, and asked me to join him. We were aware of the difficulties this would entail. It would have been preferable to start in a completely new business together, rather than have me join him, but we got together and drew up an agreement, satisfactory to both of us.

We moved into a house in Christchurch and got the two girls into the local school. However, our misgivings were justified. I think we were the only people who bought a house on the South Coast just for the summer, and then moved out. We had been gazumped on the house in Christchurch and had to obtain it by putting in a sealed bid. We got it, but only by paying more than the original price. However, we had redecorated it, and fortunately we made a profit when we sold it.

We put our names down for a house which was being built on an estate in Prestbury, but the builders kept changing the completion date, and we were forced to rent a flat from a friend. Consequently, when we moved back, we had to hire a van and put most of our furniture into store. What a heap this van was! Only one brake was working. It meandered all over the road, and we were convinced we would never reach Cheltenham. However, we did, and then we had to return for the rest of our possessions. We loaded them up into the speedboat, which doubled as a removal van, sedated the dog and the cat, packed the three children in, and set off.

There were some industrial premises for sale in Keynsham Street, Cheltenham. They were phenomenally expensive for the time, and consisted of a large workshop and a yard with open storage all round, plus a neglected building which had been three houses joined together, with an adjacent yard. It was bigger than we would need, but we knew of a plumber who wanted to move to something larger than he already had. Together we had a look at it and agreed to split it. We would have the workshop and half the yard, and he would have the rest. He had the wherewithal to improve the neglected building, and he also transformed the open storage into small individual units for letting out, applying for planning permission after he had done it. He was a slippery customer. He twisted me out of one of the units by threatening to back out, and he knew I was desperate. Still, *c'est la vie!*

In order to buy our half, we had to get a bank loan. We had already put some of our money in John's business, to buy his new premises, and it was difficult to extract it, so he agreed to pay a low rate of interest for it, and we had to go and see our bank manager. He was supposed to be a friend, but he insisted on collateral three times the size of the loan, including a second mortgage on our house, the Jag, and various insurance policies. We tightened our belts more than we thought possible, gritted our teeth, and paid that loan back within a year, much to his astonishment. One up to us! Ha, ha.

In the meantime, the builders were still delaying on the new house, so we went to see a 1930s house, which had come up for sale. There were several contracts out on it, and they said whoever signed first could have it. We signed that day and have been in it ever since. When they eventually finished the new house, we sold it, as house prices had gone up.

About this time, MOT testing came in, and I decided to become an MOT testing station. It cost me a packet of money with all the equipment we had to have. When it was all fitted, we called the Ministry to advise them we were ready for a final inspection. The man came out and passed everything until he looked at the strip light above the hoist. It was hanging down about an inch on one side, so I said, "I'll put my ladder up and adjust it now."

"No, you won't," said the official, "you re-apply when the job is done."

I was fuming. A job that could have been done in two minutes took four days until they once again came out and passed it all, so I could start testing cars at last. The official's last remark on the way out was an absolute insult. It was: "Of course, Mr Smith, when you're testing a car, YOU ARE ONE OF US."

I thought, "You are living in cuckoo land, mate. If I ran my business like you operate, I'd soon go bust."

I had to go on a day's course in Birmingham periodically, which was a complete waste of a man's working day. There were other garage people there, who were all in agreement that it was a waste of time.

I started testing when MOT testing first started, and in those days you could test a car using jacks. It was the only way with old cars. The things one tested in those days were brakes, lighting and steering. That was all.

Brakes in those days were pretty useless. Some were operated by cable and rod, and there were a few cars with hydraulics, which were almost good. One problem was the cylinder, which pushed the brake shoes on to the drums and either became seized up or leaked, so the fluid acted like oil and grease and, of course, the brake couldn't work.

Seat belts in cars weren't invented in those days. They were only in aircraft. Car floors were made of wood, loosely fitted, so you couldn't fit belts even if you wanted to. There was no such thing as fuel emissions.

As the years went on, cars became better and better. Disc brakes came in, power assisted brakes, seat belts were fitted as standard, although some older cars had seat belts fitted by a mechanic drilling holes in the floor pan and the door pillar. This was a horrible job, but it had to be done.

One lady brought her car in for an MOT. She was quite a laugh, so I knew I could have a bit of fun with her. When she came to pick up her car at the end of the day, she said, "Well, did it pass?"

"No," I replied.

"What did it fail on?" she asked.

"It failed because the nut behind the wheel is loose."

"Oh, how much is that going to cost me?" she asked.

My assistant was killing himself, laughing with his hand over his mouth.

"Well," I said, "I don't think any money will fix this."

Her face dropped and I started to smile.

She exclaimed "I'm that loose nut, am I?"

We all fell about laughing. The car had passed its test with flying colours.

Not all people were as nice as her. One or two didn't think

their cars should fail and they started giving me reasons why they shouldn't. I told them the test could save their life, but they ignored that. In fact, they tried to tell me how to do a test and things became a little heated.

I used to say to them, "Here's a form. You fill it in and send it to the Ministry of Transport and they will come out and test your car. If they do, they will probably find a few more faults that I have been lenient about."

One fellow came in with a Ford Anglia and he said he had renewed all the steering joints and it should pass. Of course he couldn't test the headlamp aim, so I adjusted them and didn't charge him (which I usually did as a goodwill gesture).

I put the car up in the air on the hoist, and the first thing I noticed was the castellated nuts, which held the steering on, had lovely red string pushed through the split pin hole and tied in pretty little bows. I continued on with the test but failed it on that point.

He came back and went mad. I pointed out that if he had used nails, I would have passed it, but what he did was downright dangerous. He continued being very abusive, so I went across and got a red certificate made out, which meant he could not move the car from my premises. He got even madder, and said he was going to get the police. So I said, "Fine, there's the door."

He went off and I locked and secured the car. After about an hour he came back, very sheepish, and asked me if I would put split pins through the holes. I said I would have done that in the first place, but I had to teach him the lesson that string is no good. He could have killed his family along with himself and other road users. I did the job, and actually he became a reasonable customer after that.

Years later, I had an experience with the Thames Valley Police. It was New Year's Day. My wife and the four children were out for the day and I had planned to visit my brother in the New Forest.

I set off at 4.30 am. Neil, my son, had fitted me a new-fangled radio-cassette player in the Jag, with knobs and buttons everywhere. I got it to play a tape, but it was playing it over and over again and I could not stop it in the dark, so I was a bit fed up.

I got to the roundabout over the motorway at Swindon, when I was stopped by a parked police car. I was determined I was not going to get out of the car, because it was freezing. There was no other traffic on the motorway or anywhere else. I wound the window down and said, "Why have you stopped me, officer?"

"We could not see if you were wearing a seat belt, sir."

"Of course you couldn't, with two headlamps coming towards you," I said.

By this time, he had his head almost in the car, sniffing gently.

I said, "No, you think I have come from a party and am drunk."

He said, "Oh no, sir, nothing like that. What is the registration number of your car?"

"I can't remember," I said, "but it is on the front and the back."

He took down my particulars, and whilst he was doing this, I noticed his partner looking round my car.

I said, "Excuse me, officer. If your colleague is looking round my car, can I look round yours?"

"What authority do you have?" he said, in a superior tone.

I said calmly, "I am an MOT tester, and IF I looked over it, I would fail it, as you have a number plate bulb out."

"The other one is on," he said. "That's all right."

"I beg your pardon," I said. "The law is that if you have two lamps, both of them have to be working."

"Where does it say that?"

"Ministry of Transport information, and the Tester's Manual," I said. "It came into force today, January 1st at twelve o'clock."

He said, "We've got a Tester's Manual in the car."

I wasn't going to get out in the cold, so I asked him to get it, which he did. He gave it to me, and I opened it at the right page, right paragraph (it almost fell open there) and I gave it to him.

He read it and said, "You've got us there, sir, but it was all right when we left the depot."

So I said, "They all say that. You are driving it illegally."

The policeman became flustered, no doubt regretting that he had stopped me.

"What shall we do?" he said.

I said, "Not me, you."

He said, "We've got a bulb in the back, but I don't know how to do it. We can get it fitted when we get back."

I think he was hinting that I should fit it.

I said, "You cannot move this car. If you do, you are breaking the law."

He said, "What shall we do?"

I said to him, "You are the one with the two-way radio. Call them up to send a mechanic."

He said, "It will be light soon, and we won't need lights."

I said, "You are still driving an illegal car and if you move it in my presence, I shall make a citizen's arrest."

I have never known a policeman so nice. We agreed that he would call up his depot, and meantime, I could do as I really wanted, and get on my way. With a policeman on each side of my car, I started the Jag up and floored the accelerator and left two black tyre marks, showing that I was angry. As I drove away, I thought, "Oh, I hope they don't lay in wait for me coming back."

My first Jag was brand new. It was wonderful, sleek, powerful, fast and quiet. My brother John heard some time before that a new model was coming out, so, as he used to sell cars down in New Milton, he ordered six of them, believing they would be delivered one a month, but the opposite happened. All six came at once. He became overwhelmed with them.

At that time, I was still a partner in their garage, having left my share of the profits from Cleeve Hill with them, to enable them to buy the New Milton garage. I had never been paid anything at all, so he decided to give me one of the Jags instead.

I kept that car well maintained and well polished. One day a good friend asked me if I would sell it to him. After a while I did, and that left me without a car, so I went to the local Jag garage and bought a low mileage white one. The downside was, it was only a 3.4 litre and I'd been used to a 4.2 litre, so I could tell the difference.

One day, Pat and the children were going to Cardiff, so they drove down the motorway until they came almost to the toll bridge. She heard an expensive noise coming from the engine, so she pulled over into a service area, and someone told her the big ends had gone. It's my belief the car did not want to go across to Wales and decided to protest.

Anyway, Pat tried to contact me, but I was out flying my aircraft and could not be contacted (more about the flying later), so she got a breakdown truck to carry the car and its passengers back home to Cheltenham. They missed the meeting they were going to, and I had a long lecture about mechanics looking after their own car, and knowing when it was about to break down.

Next Sunday we all went down to the garage to get the old engine out. As luck would have it, I'd bought a brand new 4.2 engine from another garage up North. It had been standing in my garage for about four years. You see, I intended to fit this engine when I had time. Well now was the time!

All my family and a lad called John Emmett, who came from school and worked for me in the evenings and weekends, came and helped me. He worked like a Trojan, in fact they all did. We got the engine and gearbox out, and stood it along the side of the old engine. We washed the new engine down, as it was covered with old oil and dust, as you can imagine. Then came the fiddly work of changing all the components over, as the new engine came bare. When that was done, we fitted the complete unit to the car.

John was smaller then, and it looked so funny, as John and Neil, both much of an age, could get in places that I couldn't, and they would come up from underneath the car and the engine, covered in oil and grease. I think we finished the whole job by eight o'clock. I've never changed a Jag engine so quickly. I gave John the pleasure of turning the key for the first time. She started almost at once. We were all shattered.

John Emmet at that time was still at school, but when he finished school, he came and worked for me, and trained as a mechanic. In fact now, years later, he is working for Neil in the same premises. I owed him a lot, so I taught him a great deal, plus he had a job when there weren't many jobs around. He was great, always smiling and no complaints.

I must tell you about John. We had a fleet of ice cream vans to look after and one day, after a thunderstorm, one van had hit a small flood, which turned it over onto its side. We had it lifted to the garage.

John came round when it was being unloaded. The ice cream had spilled out of the fridges and spread everywhere, still covered in hundreds and thousands etc. You should have seen John's eyes light up as he was scoffing up the spilt goodies. He stuffed himself all evening, and why he wasn't sick we shall never know. The owner of the fleet remarked that he was like a vacuum cleaner.

I had the job of jacking the van body back into shape. The windscreen had popped out, so, jacking carefully, I got the aperture dead right, so then I refitted the screen, and apart from some small dents, everything was fine and the van was out again next morning.

These vans kept me fully employed, but mostly at inconvenient times, and they would break down way out in the Cotswolds. One of them broke down at Bibury, a well-known tourist spot, and a good place for selling ice cream. I had to fit a new water pump. Unfortunately no gasket was supplied with it, so I had to improvise one out of brown paper. I stopped everyone who passed, asking if they had a pair of scissors. Eventually, an elderly lady produced a tiny pair of nail scissors, and I used those. Her husband said, "She wouldn't help me like that, but as you are a stranger, she will."

The driver who called me out the most was an elderly gentleman called Len. He would start his round, a loose term for it, and drive down narrow tracks which seemed to go nowhere, but usually had a house at the end, where they would buy ice cream from him.

It was always in these inaccessible places that he broke down, and I had to look for him. There was no satnav in those days of course. I relied on his instructions and sometimes he was miles wrong.

Anyway, late one night he was returning from his round and managed to lose the prop-shaft, which is the main eight-foot-long drive shaft, which connects from the gearbox to the rear axle, thus driving the rear wheels. He was driving down Cleeve Hill at the time. The noise and vibration must have been tremendous, but, when asked, he said he didn't hear a thing - not surprising, as he was a terrible driver. He could wreck anything. He said he accelerated at the foot of the hill, the engine revved, but he wasn't going any faster.

I went out to him, and retraced his steps, so to speak. I found the shaft lying in the middle of the road, with cars swerving around it. I laid under the van, and bodged the shaft back on, and then repaired it properly the next day, when I could get spares.

My best customer of all was a baker's firm, called Leopolds, long established in Cheltenham. I looked after a fleet of vans and cars for them for over 30 years. In that time, I never left them without a van for deliveries next morning at 4 am. Some nights I worked nearly all night.

They were very nice people to do work for, but once again the drivers were awful. The fleet of vans were changed every two years. They ended up with dents of all sizes, but the engines and running gear were in first class condition.

Every change of van I had to learn about pretty quickly. If the manual said "use a special tool" it made my brain go into overdrive, as I thought that instead of buying a tool for hundreds of pounds, I could improvise and make something that would do the job just as well.

Over the years I made quite a lot of tools of one kind or another, but all were lost when we had a break-in during the night. They even stole a customer's new car to take the tools away in. This was a blow for me, because I hadn't any tools to work with next day. I had to turn customers away - never known before in my garage.

We had several break-ins over the years, as these people were after MOT certificates. One time I arrived for work and had a feeling that something was wrong, but it wasn't until I went into the stores where the safe was kept that I saw, lying on the floor, my welding torch, still burning. They had started cutting into the safe door, but after cutting through the thin outer metal, they hit solid concrete and gave up. Little did they know that even if they had got through the concrete there would have been an explosion which would have forced the lock deeper in, and only complete destruction would have got the contents out.

To gain access to the garage, they had removed a skylight in the roof. Once again I reported it to the Ministry, and once again I was treated like a criminal.

Another time, four young men drove into the garage with an old car. They jumped out, shouting that the car was on fire. Smoke was billowing out from under the bonnet, but I thought it was a bit fishy when, as I lifted the bonnet, one of the men asked to use my toilet. I said yes, as I looked at the engine and noticed that all over the exhaust manifold was clean fresh engine oil, smoking like mad.

I said to the driver, "Have you just topped up the oil in the engine?"

"Yes," he said, "I spilled some. Could you clean it off for me?"

I did so, and by this time the other man had come back and got into the rear of the car and kept saying, "Let's go."

I thought it strange, because they reversed out very fast. I went straight to the safe, and sure enough, the certificates and the embossing stamp had gone. It was partly my fault as I should have locked the safe, but when they drove into the garage, I was filling out a certificate, and as soon as I heard the word "fire" I threw everything into the safe and slammed the door, but did not lock it with the key.

The Ministry man came and grilled me. You could tell he didn't believe me, and once again made me feel like a criminal. However, every garage man dreads the word "fire" and goes into action immediately.

One day, someone told me of a vehicle auction selling ex-Army vehicles and equipment, including cars with low mileage. I thought this might be an opportunity to buy a couple of cars to renovate and re-sell.

There certainly was a large number of cars, but nothing really suitable for me. Up there, I met a couple of other garage owners, and we compared notes and sympathised with each other about customers who expected a big job done in a short time.

"I've got the perfect invention," said one.

"Share your idea with the rest of us," we said.

"Well," he said, "I am going to have a low board on wheels, which attaches to the underside of the car. I am going to lay on it and repair the car while the customer drives around. Then he won't have to leave his car at all!"

We all laughed sarcastically.

On one occasion, a TV aerial company had their big van break down on the main A40 in Northleach. It was dark and raining and the half-shaft had come loose, giving no drive.

There was no by-pass then, and the vehicle was on the side of a bend. Of course, it had to be the offside half-shaft. I set to work to remove it. The wheels were in pairs, so I had to get them off while dodging the traffic, water dripping down my neck and off my hair and the end of my nose.

As usual, the police came to investigate.

"You are causing an obstruction," said the constable.

"Well, it's undriveable," I said. "I can only suggest that if you are feeling strong enough, we can try pushing it up the road. Of course we'll have to lift it as well, because look - the wheels are off."

He looked at the size of it, gleaming in the wet, with little rivulets of water streaming off it, and decided he was needed urgently elsewhere, and left me to my task.

I got it done eventually and made my way home, tired and wet, and wondering why I had gone into the garage trade. Instead of the long hours, rain and mud of the farmer, I now had the long hours, rain and oil of the mechanic.

Andrea and Michele had been having riding lessons since they were small and asked if they could have a pony. Now that they were teenagers, I thought it would be good for them to care for an animal, and be a nice interest for them if I could manage to arrange it.

I had a customer living on a small farm in Prestbury, who was interested in horses. He said he would have the pony on one of his fields with his horses and keep an eye on it, if I would maintain his vehicle. He even found a nice 14 hands skewbald pony called Spice. It was quite a satisfactory arrangement. The girls had a good time and went to a few gymkhanas with it.

We acquired a broken down horsebox, which I thought I could repair and improve with new wooden sides and floor. The trouble was I used very thick wood and this made it so heavy that the 1300 Escort had a job to pull it, and it was pretty nerve-racking for Pat. It really needed Hercules to lift the draw bar and connect it to the car, and when it was done, the car took on a different attitude. The front came up, and the back went down, and the car just about managed to pull it.

When Andrea reached 17, driving age, the pony had to go. It was with a heavy heart that the girls said goodbye to him, but he went to an experienced horsewoman, who planned to teach him to draw a trap. Their grief was diminished a little by the realisation that cars have reliable brakes, whereas horses do not.

11

USA Visit

It all started when I received a letter from Billy Liner suggesting that I make a trip to the States and stay with him and his family. I hesitated for a while, because my new baby son, Neil, was only a couple of months old. However, it was the chance of a lifetime. After all, I had worked very hard, and another American customer worked for the American Embassy in London, and she got me a visa. I booked a freelance mechanic to replace me at the workshop to assist Joe, the German mechanic, and off I went.

It was very exciting to fly in a Jumbo jet in those days (1970). It took us eight hours to fly across the Atlantic to Dulles Airport in Washington.

As soon as I arrived, the American customs recognised me immediately as an international criminal. They opened my suitcase and searched it thoroughly. Of course they found nothing, and handed it to me to repack. I spent ages trying to get everything back in. Pat had packed it meticulously, providing everything I would need for the three weeks into one suitcase, and using the two girls to sit on it and force it in. I could not possibly equal this, and in desperation I handed it back to the customs official and told him to do it, as it was beyond me. I walked away from it, desperately hoping I would see it again, but having my doubts.

However, it did turn up at my final destination. From Dulles, I had to board a plane to Dallas in Texas, another eight hours flying. We had arranged for Billy to meet me. After I reclaimed my bags, we started our journey to Fort Worth. Billy said it was just down the road. That took us four hours! When we got on the freeway, the road just disappeared into a dot on the horizon, it was so flat and so straight. The speed limit at that time was 60 mph - rather silly because the freeway was practically empty. At any rate, we arrived at Billy's house and I was greeted by Alice, Billy's wife. We had a meal and I fell into bed.

Next morning, I was woken by a clattering noise. I found out later that it was the air-conditioning system. It was opening and closing the vents in the ceiling, and setting up the most awful din.

After a wash and shave, Billy said we would go out and have breakfast. This seemed very funny to me, but seems to be the normal thing there. We arrived at a diner, went in, sat down. The waitress came along and asked what we wanted. One of the items on the menu was steak. I love steak, so I ordered it. When it came, I was astonished at the size - it overhung the plate and was about two inches thick. Lovely! Whilst having breakfast, the locals started to come in, and the first thing they did was to take their guns and lay them on the table in front of them. It was a little like the Wild West. Even the Sheriff and his men came in, and removed their guns. I got quite nervous but my fears were overcome when we managed to walk out unharmed.

Billy was a master sergeant in the American Army and he took me into Fort Worth and introduced me to some of his friends. They asked me all sorts of questions about England. I tried to make it as interesting as possible, but they seemed to be under the impression that everybody knew the Queen personally. I had to apologise and say, "No such luck."

After that, he took me around the PX store and it was loaded with all sorts of food, clothes, garden implements, even cars, but the food really caught my eye. We bought a lot - I can't remember what now, but I think it was burgers, wieners, etc, because we were going fishing.

The old Camero that I had rebuilt from a smash was still owned by Billy and I ended up doing a job on it. Billy was over 20 stone and he had broken the back of the seat, so I had to take it out and strip it out of its upholstery and then find a place to get the frame welded.

We found a small workshop and asked if he could do some welding for us. He declined, by saying he was too busy, so I said to him, "May I use your welding plant and pay you for it?"

He agreed readily, because he said he wasn't a welder, so to me that was lovely. I set to, and welded and strengthened the frame sufficient for Billy's weight. After I had finished the welding, the mechanic came across and looked at it so that he could assess how much to charge us. He was impressed with my welding and offered me a job there and then!

He asked me a lot about England, in particular about our cars, which he called "titchy little squirts." Of course out there, they were great gas-guzzlers, about a mile long and half a mile wide.

Billy paid him and I went back and refitted the seat, and all was well.

Next day, we went to visit Billy's parents, also just down the road - in the state of Louisiana! This also took nearly all day to get there, but I must admit we did stop off at a couple of bars/diners. We eventually got to his parents home.

His father was a haulier, with a huge lorry, and his mother's speciality was cooking grey squirrel, which put me off instantly, because we look upon them as tree rats, but they see them as a great delicacy. After the meal, Billy's father went outside to check over his lorry, and I asked if I could go with him. Getting up into the cab made you feel you were so high up you were in danger of falling out. Once inside, it looked huge. Behind the driver's seat was a compartment where the driver could sleep, very luxurious. They had everything in there, a fan, a bed, microwave, TV and air-conditioning. When you sat in the driver's seat looking along the bonnet, it was breathtaking; it was so long and wide.

I wondered then how those drivers could drive those things and reverse them into tight places, because looking into the side mirrors along the side of the vehicle, it seemed to be about three miles long.

Then I asked to look at the engine, and much to my surprise, the bonnet and the front wings were all made from fibreglass. He lifted these off so easily, I said to him, "Why do you have this thin fibreglass on these lorries?"

He said, "If you have an accident and you smash them, they only take five minutes to change."

That evening, Billy took me to a very busy bar. We were talking to each other loudly, because of the noise. Someone must have heard my Gloucestershire accent, because all the ladies came crowding round me, saying, "Say some more in

161

English." I think I must have had the reddest face ever, because they wouldn't leave me alone all evening. I think I lost my voice in the end. It was difficult to escape, because no one was allowed to walk away from the bar carrying a drink. You had to call a waiter to do it.

Meanwhile, Billy was laughing his socks off, because he could see how uncomfortable I was. I didn't live that one down throughout the holiday.

Next morning Billy said, "OK, let's go fishing." The manmade lake wasn't very far away. His parents owned a mobile home right on the lakeside. It had all the conveniences and was extremely comfortable. Billy got the boat out and fitted on the outboard motor. Away we went.

Most surprising to me, the lake opened up and standing in all this water were dead trees everywhere. Apparently, they had dammed a little stream and flooded the valley. It seemed such a shame to me to see all these beautiful trees dead. Any rate, we stopped the engine and out came his fishing kit, which I remembered back on the River Severn. Now I could see the point of it. The lake was stocked with all different fish, and Billy gave me a rod and line and we both got down to serious fishing. Billy was catching fish as if it was going out of fashion , and it took me about an hour before I caught my first tiddler. After that, I was pulling them out the same as him, and it became very boring.

We were sitting in the middle of the lake in the blazing sun and it made me feel quite ill. The sun was just setting when we reached the bank and the mobile home. Billy set to, and de-scaled and gutted the fish we had caught. Then he got the barbecue out and started cooking. All the spices he could find were used to dust the fish. When I ate one, it was beautiful.

I am not really a fish eater, but these were so fresh and so expertly cooked.

The following day, he and a couple of friends of his took me into the forest to shoot squirrel. I thought it was funny why I was sitting on the door side of the truck with two other guys sitting in the middle, but he said, "Out you get, Mike," so I obliged and was promptly almost eaten by huge mosquitoes. I heard them all laughing at me, when Billy emerged from the truck with an aerosol can, and sprayed my face and hands.

He kept quite close to me while we were walking round looking for squirrels. He lent me a gun, although I hated guns of all descriptions, but I looked the part. He told me that if I heard a dry rustling noise, I should stand still, because it would most likely be a rattler. We carried on walking. Billy was about 20 yards away from me, and we had walked for about an hour, when I did hear a rasping, rattling noise. I was petrified, and had no trouble freezing, as he had told me.

The next thing I knew, an arm and a pistol came over my right shoulder. There was a loud bang, and the rattling and rasping stopped. I said to Billy "I didn't see it, I only heard it."

He said, "Yes, just look at it now, it's dead. It just fits in with the undergrowth." He said if I had gone an extra couple of yards, I would have been within striking distance.

I thought I would rather go on strike at this time, and from then on, for the rest of the day, I was absolutely scared to put one foot in front of the other. I don't know how many squirrels they bagged. I made a token gesture by lifting my gun and firing here and there at nothing. I think I hit a couple of trees, but they would be hard to miss, being so close together.

*

We spent a very enjoyable time in Louisiana, hunting, shooting and fishing - or at least Billy did. We even walked alongside the Mississippi River, where Billy ran his hand along the water beside the bank, where it was possible just to lift a fish out.

Then it was time to return to Texas. We had a couple of drinks and then set off on the freeway, which disappeared in a straight line into the distance through rather boring desert and scrub. Our speed crept up, although we knew they were very strict on the speed limit.

We idly noticed a helicopter above us for a while, but took no notice, until suddenly we saw a police car straddling the empty road ahead of us. The policeman flagged us down and we stopped. Billy told me, out of the corner of his mouth, to say nothing. The policeman approached us from behind, with his hand on his gun. "What's your hurry, bud?" he growled.

Before Billy could answer, I spoke up. "Cor, a real American policeman!" I said.

"Who are you?" he asked.

I explained that I was English and was fascinated by the American police, and the fact that they all carried guns. There followed a long conversation about how it was possible for British police to operate without guns, which he could hardly believe. He even took his gun out to show us, and we ended up taking pot shots at the cacti!

Eventually, he let us go with a nod and a wink, and advised us to be careful in future. Billy couldn't believe our luck.

Back in Texas, I awoke early one morning, and decided to go for a walk and look at the neighbourhood.

I had not gone far before I was aware of a car crawling along behind me. I turned round, and a policeman got out and began to question me. Apparently, it is unheard of for anyone honest to go for a walk in the States. I had to explain again about what it was like to be English. Goodness knows what impression the police have now about the English. Anyway, they let me go, obviously deciding that I was mad but harmless.

Billy decided to take me for a visit to the Southern Comfort distillery. This was an eye-opener. It was started by black people, and is still run solely by them. As we walked in through the door, an overpowering but lovely odour hit us. Water for the plant was drawn from the old Mississippi. It was extremely polluted with dead animals and everything else you can think of. They had a wonderful filtration plant, fortunately, and we did drink our free sample. They asked if we had Southern Comfort in England, and I said no, but I was working on it! And sure enough Billy had managed to buy a bottle back in England. Today, of course, there is plenty of it.

He also took me to see a diamond field. This was a huge desert area which had been used for open cast diamond mining. They had removed all the reasonable-sized diamonds and it was open to the public to pick up any tiny ones they could find. You had to produce them when you had finished and sign a piece of paper to say you were not going to sell them commercially.

Taken that I was English, they would not let me have any, so I had to hand them in. I said to the official, "Is there anything to say I can't give them to my friend?"

He said, "I have never heard of anyone giving diamonds away to their friends, but you are English. I will let you do it."

I thought they were silly laws.

The time had come for me to depart back to England. On the internal flight from Dallas to Dulles, it was the time when

America had a beer festival, so the aircraft was loaded with cans of beer.

All the passengers were very nice to me, realising I was English, and one Australian offered to buy me a drink because we won the rugby, apparently. I don't know, I don't follow it, but I didn't let on, and got a free beer. The falling-down water was taking its toll amongst them. I, too, was feeling a bit inebriated, but I was fortunate, not being much of a beer drinker.

During this session, I pulled out a load of English change (pre-decimal). This aroused interest amongst the Americans, and it ended up with me exchanging two shilling pieces for dollar bills, a huge profit, but they cleaned me out of all my change. When I got back to England I changed the dollars back into pounds.

I had not slept for 24 hours, and on the train back home, I fell asleep, and almost missed my station. Pat picked me up, and then I heard the list of everything that had gone wrong while I was away.

She had a puncture on the first day, the temporary mechanic never turned up, she had to go down to the workshop every day, etc. However, Joe had coped very well. I vowed never ever to go off again, because the tongue pie and cold shoulder was a bit too much.

12

Heading Skywards

In 1978 another son, Chris, joined us, much to Neil's delight. Not only was he not outnumbered by sisters, he also had a future footballer to join in his enthusiasm for the game. Neil had waited eight years for this and as soon as Chris could toddle he was taught to kick a ball, and proved to be just as besotted by the game as Neil. Chris was born with long legs, and they continued to grow. Sometimes I thought my wife must be standing him in a bucket of manure overnight.

He is brilliant at drawing cartoons, and drew several of his friends at school, which his mother has saved. He is also very amusing and is often called on to be best man at weddings, due to his witty speeches, and his way of greeting guests to exclusive venues with the words, "Welcome to my pad."

For many years I had been friends with Eric Burke, a scrap metal merchant. Eric was addicted to flying and this addiction had spelt disaster for his several marriages. Be that as it may, it was about this time that Eric asked if I would like to go for a little flight in his powered glider.

Well, I don't know if it was Eric's dazzling personality or the thrill of the flying, but I fell for it. He took me along and introduced me to John Cole, who was the chief Flying instructor at the Cotswold Aero Club. This turned out to be my second home, according to Pat. I really took to John Cole. He was always laughing, and was very modest about his exploits and experiences.

John Cole was fully booked up at that time, so I had to wait for lessons. Meanwhile Eric had seen a friend who knew of a Piper Cub that was for sale. I should have realised he wanted a partner. Be that as it may, we drove all the way up to Barton Airfield, near Manchester, and we bought it. Not knowing a thing about aircraft, we went back to Cheltenham and told John Cole that we had bought a Piper Cub.

Straightaway he said, "Lessons can start this weekend." He loved old slow aircraft.

We collected it from Manchester and brought it back to Staverton. John Cole was all over it. You see, he used to fly old Dakotas during the last war and was involved in the Berlin Airlift, when coal and flour were carried to the people of Berlin when the Russians cut off all roads and there was only one corridor for aircraft.

Of course, John made us all laugh because flying back one day from Germany he thought he was sickening for something, because he could hardly move the controls. They were so stiff. When he got back and landed, he reported this and the engineers found that the flour and coal dust, mixed together with damp, had turned into concrete where it had set round the pulleys for the control cables. No wonder he couldn't move them!

The Cub reminded him of the old Dakotas, because they were both tail-draggers, ie the third wheel is fitted to the tail of the aircraft, whereas the tricycle undercarriage has the third wheel at the front - the norm for the majority of aircraft. Both the Cub and the Dakota have a wonderful safety record. John said that if I learned to fly a tail-dragger, I could fly any other plane, and this proved to be true.

Lesson Number One: This turned out to be circuits and bumps. You take off, climb to 200 feet and then to 800 feet and virtually go round in a circle and land where you took off from. You do this many times.

We took off. John sat at the back with his own controls, if needed. Well, we did the circuit all right. I lined the aircraft up with the runway and, closing the throttle, we descended to landing height. I noticed that my right hand wing had dropped, and over my headset, John was saying, "Pick it up, Mike."

He said it three or four times, but my wing was getting lower and lower, until it was about two inches off the ground. Then a calm voice said "I have control" and the wing instantly came up to where it should be.

John's voice came: "Ha, ha, you'll get the hang of it. Off you go."

So I was beating the circuit again, and my landings became second to none.

After many lessons the day came when John and I were practicing joining the circuit at 2,000 feet. We did three of these and John said, "OK, let's go and have a cup of coffee."

So we landed and John got out and made his seat belts secure on the back seat.

I was sitting there with the engine ticking over, when he said, "Off you go on your own. I'm fed up with looking at the back of your head, and your two ears that look like wing nuts. This is your first solo. You'll have lots more of these if your solo is OK."

I said to him, "I'm not ready yet, John."

He said, "Well, you're about to find out if you can do it. Don't make a mess on the runway if you crash."

This was said between laughs.

I called up the tower on the radio in fear and trepidation. They gave me clearance for take-off, I did all my checks as I was taught, and moved out onto the runway. I thought to myself, "Shall I, or shan't I?"

I don't know what made me push the throttle forward, but I found myself roaring down the runway doing about 60 mph. Before I knew it, I was in the air and that was the point of no return. I climbed away and all my fears melted away, because I had a heavy workload and didn't think of myself. I turned downwind and relaxed, and suddenly thought, "I'm up here. How am I going to get down?"

I settled down and did a textbook circuit and a textbook landing. Trembling all over, I pulled up on the apron where John had been watching me. He came running up, beaming and of course laughing, as he always was.

I opened the door and he patted me on the back and shook my hand. My confidence had returned. I still had a lot to learn, but felt I was really making progress.

When I was flying with John, he was sitting in the back singing and whistling and I thought he was not in charge of the controls, but as soon as I made a little mistake, he immediately took over, so quickly I wondered what had happened. One day, we were flying and I did something spectacularly right and he patted my back so vigorously that I was rocking back and forth and the plane started to do the same, as my hand moved the control column. John never told any of his students off. He was a brilliant instructor. If you did make a mistake all he said was, "Ha, ha, you won't do that again will you?" and he laughed like a drain.

One winter's night, instead of John having to drive over to the club house, I went to his house to take an exam. It was the first time I had met his wife, Ruby. She was lovely, bubbly and produced a large piece of cake and a cup of cocoa, and made me feel at home. Both of them laughed a lot together. After that all of us became good friends.

John was ex-RAF and he could fly anything to perfection. In fact he taught me a lot of the finer points. Navigation was the hardest part of the course for me, because you could do all the planning in the lecture room OK, but to put it into practice was a different thing altogether, as sometimes the wind would change direction and blow me off course, but we got over that eventually.

Now came my first cross-country qualifier from Staverton to Weston-super-Mare. From there I had to fly up to Halfpenny Green near Birmingham.

It was a devil to find the airfield, as it was surrounded by woodland. I was searching everywhere for this blasted field, and panic was setting in. I scanned the area for the last time before planning to do a 360-degree turn and fly home, when I looked down and to my amazement found I was directly over the airfield.

Feeling quite pleased with myself, I joined the circuit and reached the downwind section. I did all my radio calls correctly and proceeded with my final approach. Well, that was fine, but with a Piper Cub, one can't force it to land. One had to fly along the runway about two foot above it, with the control column being pulled gently back and back, as one waited until the plane decided to stop flying and do a perfect three-point landing.

Well, this time I was on finals, when the call of nature was calling me, so I did a rather fast approach. The Cub didn't like that because the front wheels had balloon tyres fitted and they tend to bounce just a little. This time they did just that. I think I did four landings at once. Never mind, no one was looking. I got my papers signed and climbed back in the aeroplane, and opened the paper to see what the air traffic controller had written. It said, A VERY GOOD LANDING. I didn't think so. I think he must have been looking the other way when I touched down.

I took off again to fly back to Staverton. By this time it was starting to get dark, and it was a little bit worrying as the Cub could only do 60 mph. Even at full bore she could only reach 70 mph and with a head wind, the ground speed was down to just 25-30 mph. Never mind, I got back just as the runway lights came on.

One Sunday morning I was in the Club, when one of my friends came up to me and asked if I was going flying. I looked out of the window to see fog was covering the airfield, so I said quickly, "If the birds are walking, I'm not pushing my luck. They are better pilots than you and I."

After completing all my exams, I got my licence, and from then on I was off all over the place. Eric and I went places together, like to the Isle of Wight for a cup of coffee and then back home. Bit daft, wasn't it?

Eric was a glider instructor at a small field at Bidford-on-Avon, Worcestershire, and one evening we were flying up from Usk. I was sitting in the back and Eric was captain at that time. All of a sudden, the throttle was closed and the plane was circling in very tight turns. I should have expected it. He had found a thermal, which is hot air rising very fast. The plane was lifted to 8,000 feet in a matter of minutes, without any power from the engine at all. We were at that time over the Forest of Dean. We broke out of the thermal and managed to glide all the way to Staverton, losing very little height, until we reached the airfield. We landed and congratulated ourselves on saving petrol.

When I took my cross-country qualifier, there was a very nice young man called David Martin and he was just completing a more advanced course with John. We became good friends and I took him flying with me in the Cub.

One hot summer evening we took off and headed North with all my maps and papers. It was illegal to fly without a map, so these were stacked on the back shelf in easy reach. Well, it seemed to get hotter and hotter inside the cabin, so, big twit that I was and still am, I decided to open the side window, and instantly the maps, papers, and other things left the aircraft at very high speed never to be seen again. I don't know why we laughed so much because I had to buy a new aviation map, which was very expensive. Nevertheless, we still had a good time 'low flying' across the fields at Evesham.

David had just passed his exams to become a pilot on the Britannia fleet. He told me he had to fly to Spain in order to do his circuits and bumps, because this country hasn't got long enough runways, except at the main airports, and they were always too busy. After a while he became the youngest captain on the fleet, flying Boeing 737s, a really exceptional achievement.

He called me on the phone one day, and invited me to fly up to Luton and fly the simulator. I asked if I could bring John Cole with me, and he didn't hesitate.

"Of course you can. He taught me all I know."

We got to Luton Airport and called the tower up on the radio. I was told to continue my course to the main runway. On reaching late finals, the controller saw us and realised that we were quite slow, being a small aircraft. So over the radio, we heard him calling aircraft which had backed up. The airliner behind us was told to go around again, and the rest of them to slow down. I landed and kept my speed up as high as I dared.

Next thing I knew, a hand grabbed the stick and said, "I have control." It was John of course and he took the aircraft about six inches off the ground again and flew the length of the runway. He turned off just in time for us to see a big airliner touching down.

I called up to thank air traffic control and to apologise for being slow. He was very nice about it, and said, "Ah well, it showed the pilots there are other hazards to be wary of, so thank you very much."

Dave was waiting for us, and took us to the simulator. As soon as we entered the cockpit, I was confronted with a mass of dials and switches. Dave had a separate console with loads of switches, etc. He sat us in the front seats and then I noticed how everything was the same as a real plane, only it was all duplicated.

David started the engines. I must say at this stage he could introduce faults from his console - very advanced for the likes of us. It was so realistic. One could even feel the joins in the concrete as we taxied out.

John did the first flight. As ever, it was a perfect take-off. Of course, he couldn't have done it if I hadn't operated the throttles. That's my excuse anyway.

David was a bit of a joker as well as me, as he had us flying out of Hong Kong airport on night vision, a notoriously difficult one. (They have a new airport now.) While we were cruising at 27,000 feet, but really still on the ground, John was enjoying himself.

When David said to him, "Can you barrel roll this?" John didn't say anything for a moment. He was thinking how to do it. Once he had it in his mind, he was off. The front of the simulator went down a little, and the fuselage leaned over at about 45 degrees. We all watched the instruments. All the important gauges turned a complete 360 degrees. When we looked at the altimeter, he had only lost 100 feet.

After his flight, David said all the pilots he knew came either very close to crashing or to a complete crash, but not with John at the controls.

Now it was my turn. John and I swapped seats and John was my co-pilot doing the throttles and the trim levers. Well, I was known as 'Straight and Level Smithy'. You see, I'm really a bad traveller when someone starts throwing the plane around. I did some tight turns and some stalls, otherwise straight and level. As I said before, the simulator was so realistic, flying just above the rooftops on the way to the Hong Kong runway. About halfway on my landing run I noticed a very large arrow on the side of a skyscraper, telling me to turn left, which I did. As I straightened up, there was the runway, and I might say I did a perfect landing.

We parked up and discussed what we had done, when David said, "Go on, Mike, fly her yourself without John."

I was taken aback a little, but I thought, "It's only a simulator, and if I crash it, it won't do any damage."

So off I went, taxiing to the runway. I lined up and gently opened the throttles, and we were heading down the runway faster and faster.

Then David shouted "Rotate!" That means I was at flying

speed, so I eased the control column back towards me, the nose came up and we were airborne.

I should have realised what was coming. As I was climbing, still looking at the runway white line, once again (yes you got it!) straight and level, David introduced an engine fire. All hell broke loose. Bells and klaxons were all going off at once. I forgot it was a simulator. It seemed just like the real thing. Sweat was dripping off the end of my nose and the palms of my hands. As for the white line, it was now on my left-hand side, about a mile away.

I operated the fire extinguisher, and that engine was now dead. We were on one engine now. I had full rudder on one way and the ailerons on the other way. David made me fly it all over the mountains and across Hong Kong again, which was difficult because of the yaw. I landed on the main runway and stopped.

David said, "Why did you stop on the runway?"

I said, "If I am landing into wind and have an engine fire, the flames are being blown backwards, not into the fuselage. If I had turned off, the flames would have engulfed the plane."

He said, "Well done. That is a new CAA ruling after a fire at Manchester Airport."

We had three hours in the simulator, but it only seemed like fifteen minutes. David told us that would normally cost £5,000. Both of us were really tired and very hot. We spun a coin to see who was going to fly the club aeroplane back to Staverton, and it fell to me. Thinking back, I was amazed how light the controls in the simulator were. Just one person could fly it.

One very frosty but bright day, I was in the flying club at Staverton, feeling rather bored, when an old friend walked in. We got chatting, so I asked him if he would like a ride in the Cub. He jumped at the chance, so we got the Cub out and I checked it over. We both got in and I started her up, let her warm up and then called air traffic control to get permission to taxi out to the runway and take off.

I thought it was such a bright day I would circle the airport and climb to 10,000 feet. It took no more than 20 minutes to reach that. The heater on the Cub wasn't very good at the best of times, but coming down, it was non-existent. It took me one and a half hours to get down to 2,000 feet, because if I closed the throttle, the temperature gauge went right off the scale to cold. That was no good. The controls on the Cub were very heavy, so if one had to hold it in one position for more than five minutes at a time, one got cramp. I tried side-slipping, but that was hard work. If I just pushed the nose down, she reached VNE very quickly, that is she was doing the maximum speed and it could rip the wings off, so I opted to fly in a straight line towards Evesham. On reaching Evesham, we were down to 2,000 feet, so now I could warm the engine up and get some heat inside before flying back to Staverton and land.

We went back into the Clubhouse and there were a few more people in this time. One guy knew I had been flying and asked what the weather was doing. I thought he only had to look out of the window to see what it was like, so I turned it into a joke, saying, "It's going to clear up and get wet." That caused a little titter.

I took quite a few people for flights over the years. Even with several hours under my belt, I couldn't get over the lovely views of the Gloucestershire countryside. I said to several of my passengers, "Looking at this wonderful sight, would you say this creation just came about by chance?" All of them agreed it could not. I really miss flying now when I see a light aircraft flying over.

We had a member in our club called Di Evans and he owned a little Pitts Special. Whereas I can only fly straight and level, Di can't keep it the right way up. When he calls up for permission to take off, the controller strongly emphasises, "STANDARD TAKE OFF" rather haughtily. This is a cue for Di to show us all how to twist the laws, as this little biplane has a big engine and a tiny airframe, and in the bottom of the floor, there is a window let in, so when he is climbing vertically, he can see where he is going, to comply with the law.

Di was a super guy who lived for flying. One day John and I decided to go for a little jolly, minding our own business and at peace with the world, when suddenly an aircraft appeared very close to us. Next thing he came alongside and we saw it was Di. He was grinning from ear to ear, and then he proceeded to do barrel rolls around us. Most of the time he was inverted, going over the top and under us, and finally he gave us the thumbs up, pulled the stick back and went straight up vertically. This happened several times. John and I had a private air display every time.

The time came when Eric Burke, my partner in the Piper Cub had a fall-out with his present wife, and they got divorced, so this meant the Cub had to be sold. It was a sad day all round. We had many hours of fun in the old Cub, but now it was gone.

I hired the flying club's aircraft for a while, but alas, the freedom had gone, as one had to be back on time for other people to fly them.

Meantime, there was a group of people who owned an Air Tourer. It was run by Mike Cuttell who was also a member of the club, and I had the opportunity to buy into it. This aircraft was a delight to fly, but it was only a two-seater, and I wanted a four-seater, so I kept a lookout for one.

Meanwhile, I had many hours of fun in the Air Tourer, and one day Eric, flying another plane, got to know a farmer in a village called Hook Norton. He was also a flyer and Eric arranged for our two planes to fly in to his lengthened field, ie two fields made into one.

When we were over the village, Eric called the farmer up on the radio. He answered with, "Hook Norton International here."

This was very funny to us as it was in the middle of nowhere and had no traffic. Eric landed easily, but the Air Tourer was a different kettle of fish. She was very much faster on the approach. I knew it would be tricky, but once committed to land I couldn't change my mind. At about 200 feet this field looked very small. I dropped down to 20 feet over the adjacent field in order to slow the aircraft down. I got down lower - don't ask me how low, because I was panicking at the time and couldn't look at the instruments. All I know was I was below the hedge height.

At the last moment I hauled the control column back and we hopped over the hedge and dropped down until the wheels made contact with the field. I braked like mad and came to a stop halfway down the second field. I turned round and taxied up to where Eric was parked.

He said to me, "That was a bit hairy, wasn't it?"

I had to admit it was, because my heart was going at twice the speed. Eric said that when I braked the undercarriage splayed outwards and the wheels displaced loads of earth and stones.

When it was time to leave, after a cup of tea and cakes, I looked at the field and thought I would never get out. On all four sides were tall hedges. I decided to take off diagonally across the field to give a longer run for reaching flying speed, so we pushed the plane backwards into the hedge. I started the engine, revved it up to full bore, then released the brakes. We shot off as I watched the air speed indicator. It was just below flying speed when I had to do something, as the hedge was growing fast - at least that's what it looked like.

At the last minute I hauled back on the stick and hopped over the hedge. Fortunately the next field sloped away, so I was able to drop the nose to gain speed. I was so pleased, that I did a low circuit, but very fast.

Eric, of course, had no problem as his plane was an Auster, with a tail-dragger configuration. My plane was a tricycle undercarriage, and while my craft was made of metal, Eric's was made of fabric and therefore a lot lighter.

Well, yet another divorce came around, this time in the Air Tourer group. They seem to occur pretty regularly in the flying fraternity, probably because flying is so addictive, and wives feel neglected. The plane had to be sold, so I was wingless once again.

By a stroke of luck I heard of an aircraft for sale at an aircraft engineering firm, based at Kings Clare. I went to have a look at it and fell in love with it. It was a Piper Pacer, a tail-dragger again. I've never seen such a wonderful paint job, even though it was on canvas. She was finished in cream, with the leading edges of the wings a dark maroon. She looked a picture. I bought her there and then, and when I returned home I telephoned John Cole and asked him if he would come with me and fly it back. His answer was more than just a plain "yes", so that weekend Di Evans took us down by car.

When we got there John and Di crawled all over it. They couldn't believe how lovely she was. She was pushed out of the hanger ready for the off. We did all our checks and sat inside. I noticed John scrutinising all the instruments. He said, "I wonder what this one is for, and what does that do? Never mind, we'll find out when we get airborne."

I let John fly it, as he had more experience than I did. It was a wise move, because as we reached the Cotswold Hills, we ran into a blizzard. It was a white-out as the snowy weather front moved through. There were a few gaps and we managed to see Aston Down airfield, so we headed towards it, because if necessary we could land there.

As we reached the field we noticed the Stroud valley was clear, so John turned and went for it. We got halfway down the valley straight into fog. John decided to about turn, dropping his height at the same time. We came out of the fog at no more than 100 feet and I shouted to John, "Look out John!"

He hauled back very quickly on the control column and opened the throttle fully. We must have missed the bank by about 50 feet.

John said, "That was near," and rolled about, laughing.

We got to Aston Down again, and were just about to land, when I looked down the Stroud valley and it was clear again, right the way down to the Severn valley. This time we went for it and all went well and we arrived back at Staverton. We lovingly put the Pacer into the hanger and went home to read the log books.

We found that she used to belong to the Kenya police force and at one time had been used to fly Joy Adamson of Born Free fame around that area. Two RAF pilots found it for sale and flew it all the way up Africa, across the Mediterranean to France, and home to England, making numerous stops on the way and having to obtain clearance to fly across each country - quite a marathon. She arrived back in this country only to be stripped down completely. All the canvas was torn off and new canvas was fitted in order to get a certificate of airworthiness. Then she was repainted to an incredible standard.

John Cole had had a very interesting life, and often entertained us with stories of his exploits.

On one occasion, during the last war, he was transporting a Tempest aircraft (a war plane). He was at about 12,000 feet when the engine suddenly lost all its coolant. The safety drill dictates that when there is any trouble with the engine you bale out, so John said he wound the canopy open and poked his head out.

Finding it was freezing cold, he said to himself, "Blow this. I'm not going to jump out." So he settled back in again and closed the canopy. Now he was left with a big glider.

He came through the clouds, and as luck would have it, found he was above Aston Down airfield, so he decided to land this plane on the grass alongside the runway, to avoid damaging the underside. With the engine out of action he had no power to pump the undercarriage down. He landed at the bottom of the field, of course very fast. He skidded the full length of the airfield and thought, "Where can I go now?"

He saw that the gate at the end of the runway was open, so he managed to steer it through the gap and stop in the ad-joining field. He had a rollicking from the station commander because he did not radio in with his position. He said, "When you are having a heart attack, radioing in is the last thing on your mind."

However, John had the last laugh, because he was awarded the Queens Commendation for his action.

On another occasion, he went to visit a friend in another RAF airfield. He noticed that there was a Spitfire standing there doing nothing, so he asked his friend if he could take it for a spin, which was agreed.

John's little devil horns came out of his head, and he flew back to his home base, and did a beat-up of the airfield and runway, flying very low and then flicking it over as he passed the control tower, so that they could not get his number. He did several runs, and felt elated at his exploit.

He went back to the Spitfire's base, returned the plane, and went back to his own base. He was greeted by his commanding officer saying to John, "There was a fool over here, beating up the airfield. We tried to get his number, but he kept turning it on its side so we could not read it. If I ever find out who he is, I shall get him court-martialled."

John sympathised with him. On the last day, John got demobbed, and went to see the CO to say goodbye, and he said, "By the way, do you remember that fool of a pilot who beat up this airfield?"

The CO said, "I shall never forget him."

John said, "It was me," and left quickly.

John was flying Dakotas in the Middle East during the latter part of the war. He had a detail to fly a group of nuns to a safer destination. He was allocated to fly with the captain, and John was the co-pilot. The nuns duly boarded the plane, immaculately dressed. They all took their seats, and the plane taxied out and took off.

John was navigating, when they hit a bad patch of turbulence. The plane was being thrown about all over the place. They reached their destination and the pilot managed to line the plane up with the runway and continued his run, being buffeted about. After a difficult landing, he parked up, turned the engines off, and said to John in a very loud voice so that everyone would hear, "That was a TERRIBLE landing you did, Cole. I will recommend you for some circuits and bumps."

Poor John took the blame, although, as he said, "I didn't even get the chance of holding the control column. I didn't get the chance to complain because the captain was a higher rank than me."

He went back to open the doors, and staggered back because the immaculate nuns were now dishevelled. Some had been very ill, and all of them were very green. Their habits were awry, and they looked much the worse for wear.

John had always wanted to fly in one of the huge gliders used in the war to invade Germany. He made enquiries of the commanding officer of the gliding section, who said he would bear it in mind, if the opportunity should arise.

An old Dakota was used to tow the gliders up. At the required height, the glider would detach itself from the Dakota. The Dakota would then go back to the airfield and land, while the glider commander put the student through his paces. Well, at this time John was teaching a student in a simulator how to fly blind by navigating with instruments. The student had a very hard workload and was expected to be in the simulator for some time.

A young RAF man came running in and said to John, "If you can come now, you can have a ride in the glider."

John said, "How long will it take?"

The fellow said, "Oh, no more than half an hour."

So John looked at the simulator, and noticed it was rocking from side to side and backwards and forwards, and he thought, "He is having fun. He will be all right for half an hour."

With that, he made his way out to the glider. He was ushered in and sat down and strapped himself in. Then they were off. The grass field was rushing by, and they were soon airborne.

Suddenly, the hawser broke and the student pilot had nowhere to go, so he landed in a field of standing wheat. Local people came running to see what had happened, and although the glider had done almost no damage to the wheat, the crowd of people soon trampled it flat.

Each of the crew had to fill out an accident report, including John, so two hours later they arrived back at camp.

John rushed back to the simulator, and there was the poor guy, still in there, calling John all the names under the sun and sweating like mad. He said to John afterwards, "I thought I wasn't getting things right, and with punishment in mind, you kept me doing it over and over again."

Who could be mad with John? They both laughed about it later, time and time again.

One day, John's luck gave out. He was instructing a student, when the fuel pump broke down just when they got to about 100 feet The engine suddenly stopped and John took over quickly.

He decided to land on top of some fruit trees in an orchard. He did his best, but ended up with the plane upside down, and John and his student hanging in the safety harnesses.

They were taken to hospital and John was found to have a broken femur. The surgeon patched him up with long steel rods, which were eventually removed, and they gave them to

John, who showed them to us and made us feel queasy. I think he did that on purpose.

I took the Pacer to an air display, and one chap showed a lot of interest in it. I didn't think much about it at the time, but this man managed to get my phone number, and constantly rang me. Sometimes he would ring three or four times a day. He wanted to buy the Pacer, but I didn't want to sell and told him so several times.

However, he wouldn't take no for an answer. He carried on wearing me down and down, until I caved in. I couldn't stand any more, but even now I still miss the old thing.

Two of my friends were professional pilots, flying executive jets. I think they felt sorry for me, as they asked if I would like to go in with them to buy an aircraft that they could use both in their spare time, and to ferry one another between airports.

I think I did more of the ferrying around. I didn't mind as I was building up my flying hours. We all looked around for an aircraft. One of them found an aircraft for sale in Dundee, Scotland. His name was David Parfitt and his job was flying people about in a beautiful new Citation, which was a twin-engine executive jet. I think it cost a few million pounds.

As for our aircraft, it was an Aero Speciale Tampico four-seater. It was very wide inside the cabin, so there would be no rubbing of shoulders, as in so many small aircraft, thus allowing plenty of room for panicking and throwing arms about.

We paid over the money and flew up to Dundee in a scheduled flight to Edinburgh. When we taxied into the terminal, we saw a tiny little plane parked up among the giant ones. It was the Tampico. Two men picked us up and flew us to Dundee in it. We completed the deal and set off on our journey back to Cheltenham. When we left Dundee, the weather was good, but after a few miles, we were in thick fog and rain.

Well, I've never flown on instruments, so David took over. I was amazed that he knew all the radio frequencies en route by heart, and got us to Birmingham flying blind. We had to divert to Birmingham because Staverton was closed. David would not land the aircraft, because he said, "Flying a large aircraft for so many years, I wouldn't like to trust myself without a bit of practice."

So it was left to me. I did my radio calls about five miles out from Birmingham. All I could see was a very large orange glow in the distance. This was the high-powered lights, which got brighter as we got closer. Eventually I could make out the runway, and I landed and parked up. We had to find a hotel just for the night.

Next morning when we woke there was no sign of fog, only a lovely summer's day. We reached Staverton in 25 minutes. When I went into the club and told my story, someone said, "Why didn't you tune into Severn Sound local radio? Your ADF auto direction finder would have taken you right over Staverton."

That's the story of my life, finding out afterwards.

I was so pleased to have a four-seater, that I took John Cole and two other friends up with me for a ride.

One hot summer's day, I took two adults and their son with me. I did my flight plan and asked them for their weight. This is most important, because if the aircraft is too heavy it will be going by road. They must have given me the wrong weights, anyway I started my take-off run and thought we were taking rather a long time to reach take-off speed. The end of the runway was racing towards us.

We reached the point of No Return and take-off speed came up just as I eased the stick back. The wheels came unstuck from the runway and we were flying, although very low. We got over the hedge and flying speed had dropped off, so I pushed the stick forward a little and raised the flaps at 25 degrees. The speed started to increase and we were climbing at last.

As we reached 2,000 feet I let fly at my passengers about giving the wrong weights. Mind you, I was to blame as well, because it was a very hot day, so of course the air was thin and I wasn't getting much lift. In cold weather the air is thicker, so there is better lift. I can remember thinking at the time, "Thank God the world is round and I can fly off the edge."

We had to get rid of the Tampico eventually, because the other two found they were not getting the time to use it as much as they had hoped, and it did not justify the expense.

Another pilot friend of mine, Mike Cuttell, had a great interest in autogyros and helicopters. The autogyro almost killed him when he crashed it, so he turned to helicopters and soon gained his licence. He was very good to me, and often took me for a flight. The only downside was that we would be flying along enjoying the countryside, and he would say, "Are you still strapped in?"

"Yes," I would say.

"Right, I am going to do an autorotation now."

That meant taking the drive out of the main rotors and gliding it down to a pre-arranged spot. This involved going round and round in circles, losing height and when we reached the ground there were a lot of expletives, because he missed the spot he had his eye on. I thought as long as we were down, that was OK, but that wasn't good enough for him, he had to go back up and have another couple of goes until he had mastered it.

He is a very safe pilot, as everything is double-checked. He is also very generous. He could not go flying on his own, because he thinks it selfish, so he takes different people up.

Looking back, I find it incredible that I had the opportunity to learn to fly and experience the unique pleasure of soaring above the earth, looking down on the patchwork of fields and hills, and the variety of scenery along the coast.

Now that I have retired and handed my business over to Neil, I have been obliged to give up flying. Still, I enjoyed 25 years of it, together with the camaraderie of the flying club and the time spent beside the wood burner with a cup of coffee waiting for the weather to clear, or enjoying the efforts of learners trying to perfect their landings.

I think back to when, as a farmer's boy during the war, I watched dogfights between aeroplanes over the fields of Oxfordshire, little dreaming that one day, I too would be up there. Of course, my skill did not match theirs, illustrated by the occasion when I spotted a dear little fluffy cloud below me and decided to aim at it and sail right through it. I lined the aeroplane up at it, kept my eye on it and dived, only to miss it by about 500 yards! There it was - floating prettily over to the side, seeming to mock me.

None of this flying would have been possible if it wasn't for my darling long-suffering wife, Pat, putting up with it and listening to the stories of my exploits.

* * *